# Forward Progress

## Confessions from a Rookie College Football Official

Discover Proven Methods to Get Noticed, Move Up and Improve
Your Officiating Skills

## Todd Skaggs

www.profootballreferee.com

# Todd Skaggs

Cover design by Candice Neal. www.createdbycandice.com

Visit our website at www.profootballreferee.com for more information on Todd Skaggs or how to improve your football officiating.

ISBN: 978-0-578-06163-4

Published in the United States of America by

Profootballreferee.com, LLC

470 Blossom Ridge Drive

Shepherdsville, KY 40165

**Attention: Businesses and Professional Organizations**: Quantity discounts available on bulk purchases of this book for educational, gift purposes, promotional, or as premiums for increasing magazine subscriptions or renewals. Special books or book excerpts can be created to fit specific needs. Contact the author at todd@profootballreferee.com. You can also call 502-215-0409 for more details.

# *Table of Contents*

Todd Skaggs

## *Acknowledgments*

This book has been a labor of love. From a day dream in December to what exists in the pages that follow, writing this book has been both tremendously challenging and incredibly rewarding. I set out on a mission to discover what the Matt Austin's and John McGrath's of football officiating knew that I didn't. How could I learn from those that blazed the trail ahead of me? Were there secrets to making it to the highest levels of this avocation, some little-discussed, seldom revealed shortcuts I might put into action? What I found amounts to hard work, humility, commitment and the ever-present helping hand.

The list of people deserving of my thanks is long and distinguished. So many people have put their signature on this work, without their insight and inspiration; the resulting content would be lackluster at best.

The order is not important, the weight of my gratitude is: Ken Rivera, Dick Honig, Jim Jackson, Gerald Austin, Vic Winnek, Doug Rhoads, Tony Michalek, Tommy Moore, Jim Augustyn, Gary McCarthy, Grant Jackson, Allen Baynes, Rogers Redding, Gary McCarthy, Matt Austin, Chuck Russ, Kavin McGrath, Johnny McGrath, Bob McGrath, Ron Baynes, Butch Stovall, Fuzzy Klusman, Jon Dawson, Tim Bryan, Roy Potts, Stan Weihe, Harold Mitchell, Billy Alton, Wilbur Hackett Jr., Bill LeMonnier, Don

Lucas, Doug Rhoads, Greg Waybright, Wally Todd. Any omissions are the fault of the author.

To the Kentuckiana Football Officials Association –There is no finer group of football officials in the US and I'm proud to be a member.

To my road-trip brethren, Meddie Kalegi and Ryan Kendall, I'll take the field with you anywhere.

Special thanks to Mike Carey for taking the time to reply to a short piece of "fan mail" from this fellow official and telling me you liked my book idea. I'll not soon forget that phone call. Sometimes it just takes a nudge in the right direction to get a snowball rolling downhill...

To Steve Joest and Jim Gutterman – I will never forget our tailgate conversation following a Bullitt Central JV game. Your encouragement and advice made all the difference to a green second year official.

To John Oslica and Paul Heavrin for telling me to go for it.

Billy Alton – thank you for giving me a chance.

My daughter Emerald and my mother Nancy, for believing.

Finally, I must thank my wife Kim for her unwavering support and encouragement as I've pursued my dream of officiating football at the highest level. Family support has never been in question. Best call I ever made.

Last but certainly not least, to my grandmother, Barbara Nell Cross, who always told me I should write a book. I finally took your advice.

## *Introduction*

—◆━━━━━━━━━━━━━━━━━━━━━━━◆—

*The one thousand mile journey begins with a single step.* --Chinese proverb

D o you still get goose bumps when the band plays the National Anthem on a cool fall Friday night? Do you dream about walking out into a stadium filled with 70,000 raving fans on a Saturday afternoon? Maybe you have set your sights on officiating a middle school play-off game, a high school State Championship, an NCAA Bowl game or even the granddaddy of them all; the Super Bowl. Perhaps you just desire to work your local youth league each weekend or get a full varsity schedule. Regardless of your intentions or aspirations, if these statements ring true, this book was written with you in mind.

This book is for those officials who do not accept average or mediocre. Are you always seeking continuous improvement? Are ever satisfied with just getting by, achieving status quo? Do you strive to improve every snap, every game, every season? If any of the above resonates, then you will be among good company. This book was written with you, the football official, in mind.

Do you ever wonder why referees use the terms craft, avocation or passion when discussing what they do on the football field? You will hear officials at all levels speak of their love of the game, their passion for football, the desire to protect the integrity of the sport. At the very basic level, we enjoy the spirit of the game; we look forward to sharing the field with the players and coaches.

We relish the responsibility to be ambassadors of the game of football, to bring wisdom and leadership to the field. But most of all, we are cognizant that the game is not about the officials, it's about the players, coaches and fans. The game is *for them,* and if four quarters expire without anyone really noticing the officials then the crew's work is done. Whether it be a Friday night, Saturday or Sunday afternoon; we enjoy our role as the custodian of the rulebook, the keeper of all things sportsmanlike, the mediator of teams doing battle on the field. We proudly don the black and white stripes and we strive to leave no mark on the game, for football officials need no fanfare, no recognition or acclaim. We don't seek headlines or interviews, praise or thanks.

Officials of all walks of life, diverse backgrounds, broad geographies, and multiple generations want but for one thing…just one more game. We are the shepherds of the sheep and we accept our role with zeal and fervor.

If you are reading this book, then one would assume you have a passion for, or at the very least an interest in, football officiating. You relish the chance to get out on the field and work a good game. Who notices you isn't important. You just love the sport of football, the competition and the craft of officiating. Well, rest assured, you are not alone.

This book is dedicated to all officials, regardless of level, who desire to get noticed, move up and improve their officiating skills. At the core, I believe we can learn from those top level officials that have achieved the heights of this avocation of which the rest of us dream. We will closely examine the best officials of the NFL and NCAA, who will share with you their stories, their obstacles, and their successes. By uncovering each and every fork in the road, every decision, obstacle or victory; our respective journey's will have more meaning, be less frustrating, and provide a higher level of satisfaction. We can learn from other's mistakes and benefit from their techniques and training. There simply is no reason to embark on this journey alone and navigate uncharted waters. Those that are currently successful have left a surprisingly simple yet effective roadmap. There are really no surprises.

I can guarantee you one thing. We will discuss concepts, principles and strategies which any aspiring official can use to improve and advance. But without ACTION and APPLICATION they are just words. You must DO something! Taking action is by far the single most important component of your future development. I will not attempt to dissuade you. Success at the highest levels will require hard work and determination. There is a reason there are only 120 NFL and approximately 750 NCAA Division One officials out of an estimated 55,000 total football officials.

This fact has been reinforced over and over as I conducted the series of interviews with the best NCAA and NFL officials. It's one thing to know what you should be doing in order to be successful; it's entirely different taking action along a predetermined path and accomplishing those goals.

I am going to peel back the layers of the onion, so to speak. Together we will take a close look at the careers of some of the biggest names in football officiating. We will ask NCAA Conference supervisors about their philosophies, criteria for application and evaluation methods. We will ask everyone what it takes to make it at the top.

While I did come across a few gifted athletes or genius minds, most are ordinary people with extraordinary desire. They are largely successful with their families, their careers, their faith and it transcends their football officiating careers as well. They have all made their share of mistakes and have each experienced success on their terms. Each considers himself fortunate to have been given the opportunity and all realizing that achieving these heights is truly a collection of efforts. No islands in this crowd.

So we will listen to their stories, hear their advice, heed their warnings. We should pause to reflect on the finer points of football officiating, as they have a parallel influence on our entire lives.

If I can help you realize your respective officiating goals just one day, one game, one season sooner; this book will have been a success. By the refs - for the refs.

Just like a ball carrier attempting to reach the line to gain, this book is about **Forward Progress**.

# Zebra Tales

Dick Honig, Former Big Ten referee and current ACC observer

*I had just completed working the National Championship in 2000, Oklahoma versus Florida State. Denzel Washington did the coin flip and I was the referee, so I had to work with him, talk with him for awhile before the game and get him oriented to doing the coin flip and whatnot. After the game is completed…Oklahoma has won, our crew has had a great game. We've had no problems, everything has been smooth, we've made all the correct calls, done everything right. We get into the dressing room, we get changed and of course my family's there. My wife's there and after the game I go out to see my wife and the first thing she asked me after the game was: "Tell me about Denzel Washington!" Nothing about the game. It brings you back to how important things were.*

*I also know that I got home after that ballgame, and you don't realize how many people are watching the National Championship game, and there are tons. I probably had 300 to 400 emails about the game from friends and relatives and whatnot. It puts it in perspective. You don't think about the pressures that you're under when you're out there doing what you do, but I sure thought afterwards, "Man, if I had screwed that game up how many of those emails would have been nasty and negative as opposed to positive?"*

# Chapter 1

## My Story

I suppose you could say I came to football officiating in a non-conventional way.

From 1987-1991, I was served in the US Navy aboard the USS William V. Pratt (DDG-44) in Charleston, SC. I had always been a decent athlete although never a stand-out by any measure. I enjoyed the focus on physical fitness the Navy provided and was a regular visitor to the base gym. The ship even had an exercise bike, a weight bench and some dumbbells. Imagine trying to bench press at sea with the ship pitching and rolling about!

In 1989, the Willie V went into the yards for some overhaul work. Little did we know this would precede our required involvement in Operation Desert Storm; but that's another story. During the extended overhaul period, the ship organized a flag football team to compete in an intramural league. After our first game, I recall meeting the officials following the completion of the game in the base parking lot. Being the curious type, I wanted to know how they became officials, were they paid, why did they like it, etc. It turned out these gents were retired Navy vets and liked officiating to keep them active and out of the house. The conversation lasted an hour or so and ended with a warm invitation to join them on the field in the near future to try my hand at officiating football.

I remember my first game clearly. Wearing a borrowed shirt, hat and flag; I stepped on the field. Granted it was flag football, but halfway through the first period one of the old veterans called me in to the center of the field and said "Well, what do ya think?"

I was hooked. Now, jump ahead 14 years to 2003. I was taking a new job and moving to a new community just outside of Louisville, KY. It was June and I had been on the internet investigating football officiating associations. I thought since I really didn't know anyone in my new hometown, I might get involved with football and make some new friends.

I called the contact number for the Kentuckiana Football Officials Association and as luck would have it, I found out the rookie class training was beginning in a few short weeks. An invitation to attend a meeting was forthcoming and seven years later; I still get butterflies on opening kickoffs!

I can vividly recall my first game and still remember my first flag. It was a Catholic school youth league game on Sunday. Bruce Colpo was the veteran on the crew and refereed the first game of a two game set. My first penalty came early on by way of a false start. I was working linesman that game and in this league, the teams are on the same side of the field. Consequently the fans split the field as well on the opposite of the two teams and the linesman has the bleachers to his back.

So, back to the false start. The tackle on my side jumped and I reach down for my flag, retrieved it from its spot on the ride side of my knickers, and launched it skyward.

The flag went up, up, up and landed about thirty feet behind me at the feet of a group of fans. Now that I think about it, they didn't give the rookies a lesson on how to properly throw a flag…My wife was in the stands for my first game and I still hear about launching the rocket-flag to this day!

About midway through the first half, Bruce killed the clock and called me into the center of the field. I thought to myself, "Oh boy, what have I done now?" I jogged in to meet Bruce, my heart pounding in my throat. Fearing the worst, he gets close and says, "What in the heck are you doing over there on the sideline? Checking out people in the stands?"

I let out a deep breath, laughed and I knew that I was going to be okay. Yes, we do have fun on the football field. I'll bet you can guess what I do with our first year rookies when I'm one of the veterans on weekend youth league games?

## My Officiating Career Path

I tend to apply the same mindset I have in my career on my officiating. I like to set goals and I like to challenge myself. I don't like getting comfortable or complacent. I really enjoy pushing myself to see what I can achieve. Once I reach a goal, I almost immediately revise it with loftier expectations.

I received a first round state playoff game assignment in my third year which was also the last game of the season. I was so energized by that game, the crew with whom I worked and the ending of a great season; I decided I needed to elevate my game. I wanted to see how far and high I could take this football officiating hobby which had grown into a mild obsession.

I began paying attention to the officials that worked the big Friday night games as well as those in college conferences. Let me state that I realized at this time I was in no way ready to move up to that level, however the planner in me desired to know the requirements so I could begin planning a direct route to get there at some point in the future.

What are the local conferences? Who are the decision makers? How do they fill vacancies? Do you need to be recommended or is there an application procedure? What are the entrance criteria? I was hungry for information.

Almost immediately I met resistance. Several more seasoned officials suggested I put college out of my mind. Focus on high school they said, the college level was years ahead in the future. Be a good high school official first. The rest will take care of itself.

I took the advice although a bit disenchanted by it. I decided I must prove my worth on the field. Maybe if I worked hard enough, improved game after game; year after year, I'd get noticed by the powers that be.

Honestly, it was a bit too much chance for my liking. I would hear about college scrimmages after they were played. I'd hear about rules study groups but didn't know who to ask about attending. I also wasn't truly certain that I was good enough to officiate at the next level.

Two things happened in my fifth year that changed everything.

1.  I realized I was one of the most senior officials on most of my Saturday and Sunday youth league games.

2.  I happened upon my first mentor.

The assignors asked the general membership to send in feedback on any first or second year officials with whom you worked, so they could conduct proper evaluations and provide coaching and feedback sessions for them.

I began sending in game critiques for each first or second year official that was assigned to my games. I also began to take a personal interest in their progress and improvement on the field. Halfway through the season, I had developed a reputation as one of the guys that took his weekend officiating seriously. I provided constructive and descriptive evaluations in a timely manner. I was ultimately approached about becoming a mentor to a rookie official during the following year as a part of a new mentoring program.

Keep in mind; I actually started providing this level of detail because I wished I had received it when I was a first or second year guy. It was as simple as that. I just wanted to help the new guys improve. I did not think for a minute that it would get any attention other than from the people I evaluated. I just incorrectly assumed everyone was taking an active interest in the rookie officials.

This season also provided a great opportunity for self-reflection. When I realized I was going to be one of the veterans on the weekend games, I had to do some soul-searching. The bottom line was I didn't know the rules as well as I would have liked and now people were looking to me for answers relative to penalties, enforcements and such.

In retrospect, that little motivation was all I needed to get me going. I hit the rule book hard in year five but committed to knowing it even better in year six. I anxiously accepted the role of being a mentor to two new officials and it was a tremendously rewarding experience. That challenged me in so many ways and fueled my desire to advance my own career even more.

The summer following my fifth year, I returned to a consistent schedule at the local gym. I hit the weights pretty hard and combined that with interval training on the stationary bike. I had forgotten how much I liked going to the gym since back in my Navy days. The results were slow arriving but brought a renewed sense of pride in myself. My mantra was to look, feel and perform well in my uniform. My physical fitness was 100% within my control and I wanted to be ready for my sixth season.

Late in my fifth season, I had the opportunity to work a few games with a guy named John Oslica. John was known for this insane weekly ritual of working a Friday night varsity contest in Louisville, KY then driving to West Virgina the same night so he could officiate an NCAA Division II game in the West Virginia Intercollegiate Athletic Conference. Some might think that's completely nuts, but I still admire him for his dedication and perseverance. I did not miss the opportunity to pick John's brain on his experiences there. John was also renewing his commitment to the gym and we became good friends. Little did I know at the time that John was blazing a trail I would soon follow.

John and I aren't that far apart in age. Being a mentor isn't necessarily about years of experience. It's about providing guidance and friendship, sharing your experiences, shedding light on dark places. John opened my eyes relative to what it took to get started in college level officiating and inspired me to chart my own course.

Over the course of my sixth season, I realized that much of the information I had been seeking was residing not in books or websites, schools or locker rooms, but in minds of great football officials. This idea of interviewing top level officials to identify any commonalities started creeping into the outside edges of my mind. What could we learn from them if we just asked? What about the conference supervisors? They are making the decisions on who the hire each year. What are they seeking in candidates?

NFL legend Jerry Markbreit visited our association meeting in 2008 and spoke about his career. One story in particular stuck with me. He told us that all NFL officials receive fan mail from the NFL Headquarters if fans take the time to send it.

I must tell you that I really never paid much attention to the officials on the football field until I started officiating. But once I got the bug, I started noticing styles and habits I liked from certain NFL referees. One person in particular had the most crisp signals and detailed explanations. His movements on the field commanded respect. His presence and command of any situation was obvious to any that watched. His name is Mike Carey and if a high school official like me is allowed to have an NFL role model, then Mike is mine.

I kept coming back to what Mr. Markbreit had said about sending fan mail to NFL officials. I had the notion that I would send Mike Carey a simple note telling him about the influence he's had on me and my officiating career. I also wanted to tell him that I'd found a new reason to purchase NFL Sunday Ticket (so I could find his game each weekend). One Sunday night, I looked on the NFL website for an email address or comments section which would facilitate the letter. None existed.

I then realized in retrospect, that Jerry Markbreit had meant we should send fan mail the old fashioned way – by writing a real letter! So I did and my letter found its way to Mike's desk.

I clearly remember I was doing a bit of last minute Christmas shopping for my wife in Bed, Bath & Beyond. As I was leaving the store, my cell phone rang and a voice on the other end said, "Todd, this is Mike Carey." I paused in disbelief, "Who?"

We chatted for a few minutes and I thanked Mike for taking the time to make the call. I stressed he had no idea how much that call had made my day. Then he shocked me by saying, "well, your letter made *my* day."

In that moment I realized Mike wasn't the larger than life figure I'd been recording in my DVR. He wasn't the Super Bowl XXVII referee in 2008. (Well, maybe he really is!) He was simply a normal person who appreciated me taking the time to share my thoughts. He just happens to be a NFL crew chief in his spare time.

I took a moment to ask Mike what he thought about my book idea and if he'd be willing to be interviewed at some point in the future. He said yes and <u>Forward Progress</u> became more than an idea. That conversation on a chilly December afternoon in the parking lot of Bed, Bath & Beyond was the tipping point for me.

Fast forward to the spring of 2009. I seriously began pursuing officiating at the collegiate level. I contacted any conference close to my home seeking information on clinics, scrimmages, or other training opportunities. I sent countless emails and officiating resumes to nearby conference supervisors. I registered for EVERY possible training opportunity within a day's drive of my home. I put into action exactly what my research revealed.

I also worked on factors I could control. I started studying the rulebook in January – a first I'll admit. I downloaded tests from Referee magazine and NASO. I hit the gym and the track intent on being in shape and looking athletic in my uniform. Again…things I control

This passage has been eye-opening and rewarding. I have learned so much in the past months. So many helping hands have reached down to this humble official offering advice, guidance and a few well-placed constructive comments. To undertake this alone would have been impossible and most certainly a failure.

I have chronicled this journey via the power of social media. You can visit my blog at <u>www.profootballreferee.com</u> where excerpts of the interviews are posted along with tons of video, audio and self-help topics along with an occasional rant from the author. You may also visit me at Facebook where I maintain a ProFootBallReferee Fan Page as well as on Twitter under the Profootballref handle. You may also find the Referee Nation podcast interesting (www.itunes.com).

You are now reading the results of the past 12 months of research that started with a conversation between a Super Bowl veteran and a Kentucky high school football official. It resulted in a collection of what the best and brightest football officiating greats have to offer. I hope you enjoy what lies ahead.

# *Zebra Tales*

Tony Michalek, NFL Umpire

*Notifications for the crew chosen to work the Super Bowl weren't supposed to go out the day they went out; but they decided to do it early. I had just worked two days before. I had worked the Dallas/Giants game where the Giants upset the Dallas Cowboys and Dallas was the #1 seed. I get a call from New York, and again because I know the time, the time was like 9:37 on Tuesday morning. On Monday and Tuesday after you work a game in the NFL, the number you do not want to see pop up on your phone is 212-450-2000. That's the league headquarters and in our profession as you know, no news is good news. So if you're getting that call on Monday or Tuesday, you've got something to think about.*

*So when that thing popped up at 9:37 in the morning on January 15ᵗʰ, 2008, I said to myself "Oh-oh, this is either going to be really good or really bad." Right away I started thinking about the game. We only had a couple things. There really wasn't anything major I didn't call. I picked up the phone and he says, "Tony, Mike Pereira." He said, "How you doing?" I said to him "Why don't you tell me how I'm doing?"*

*Right away my mind as I was racing through it I was thinking this is going to be a really good call or really bad. He said, "Well, I just wanted to tell you great game on Sunday!" I'm going "Here we go! This is gonna be awesome!" Mike is the one who makes the call for the Super Bowl and I knew I had a really good year, and the year before I was rated #1 and worked the AFC Championship Game, and I had an equal year again. It was my first year of eligibility for the Super Bowl so you may not get it. He said "Well, you did a good job; we picked out a couple plays. I'll tell you, you did a good job on those." I said, "Well, you know what? It was a great crew. Mike, thanks again for trusting me with a rookie referee." I go, "We had a great time all year, it was really a wonderful crew." I went on to a couple things about the crew and gave them accolades.*

*He said, "Well, one of those guys from that crew is going to work the Super Bowl." I hesitated, and he continued "You know who that person is?" I said, "Gosh, I certainly hope you're about to tell me who."*

*"That person is you. Congratulations." So he went on to give me all the particulars about the game, and he, and I couldn't hear a word he was saying. I mean my mind was going so fast and I was so excited. He asked me sizes of shirts and then sizes of this, and I don't even recall. I gave him all bad information! He said "What size shirt do you wear?" "X-tra large, double x-tra large! Whatever size, it doesn't matter!"*

*Yeah, I gave him a bunch of bad information, so when our bag of goodies came, nothing fit! That day was one of the most exciting periods ever in my career. So I made a bunch of calls. We talked earlier about my mentors; after my family my mentors were the first ones that I called. I called the guys, my buddies, my best friends that I brought into officiating. I called my mentors to thank them. When he told me that I was working the Super Bowl I had a tremendous amount of humble gratitude for all the people that helped me. Because anytime something like that happens, you don't get there by yourself. I just couldn't help but want to call everybody and thank them.*

# Chapter 2

## Focus Factors

◆————————————————————◆

*"Dreams meet reality only when someone shows the courage to accept*

*challenges."*

What does success mean to you? This question is posed to every reader of this book and will result in a variety of answers. You will read about successful NFL and NCAA officials in the following pages who have defined success on their terms and have their priorities in the right place.

The following traits of successful officials are called Focus Factors. I believe these are common to all successful football officials. I encourage you to conduct a self-evaluation as you read through this chapter. Examine each Focus Factor and rate yourself accordingly. We are not always who we think we are. Don't worry about giving me your answers. You have to answer to yourself.

## Focus Factor #1: Motivation

There are people who have been very successful in officiating and they have a deep and meaningful love for the game. Some people are extremely competitive and they thrive on the skill of the craft and the chance to continually challenge them to improve and excel.

Many officials are often athletes and even former players. Some, me included, are former coaches. These individuals fully understand competitive athletics and what it takes to win. Officiating offers people of all walks a way to stay in touch with the game of football.

I should make one thing very clear: Money is not the reason we officiate. While game fees at the NFL and NCAA Division I level are impressive, officiating is not about the money. Game fees are taken in trade for our skill, knowledge and devotion to the game of football, but certainly not the reason we step on the field.

Not that you won't find officials that gage their status on how much money they earn by the game, or by the season. There are those that officiate ONLY for the money. But I believe if money is your primary motivator, not only will you fall short, you will also fall by the wayside. The road to the top is paved with long nights, miles of blacktop, and cramped locker rooms. There will be times when it will cost you more to get to the game that what you actually make working it.

Not that the money at the top isn't nice. Top Division I officials can take home over a thousand dollars per game and NFL officials command several times that. Even some high school games pay over one hundred dollars per game at the varsity level and there are youth league game fees nearing fifty dollars per game. The higher you go, the more is at stake and the pay rises accordingly.

Since we are on the topic of motivation, I need to spend a moment on ego. Much like money, if the primary motivating factor to be a top level football official is to be on national television signaling to the press box or rubbing elbows with future professional football players, then I suggest your motivation is misplaced. Ego driven officials show their true colors and this becomes very apparent as they begin to move up. Truly successful officials check the ego at the door. Officiating is a humbling experience and you will find two types of officials as a result: those who *are* humble and those who will *become* humbled.

**Focus Factor #2: Achieve & Believe**

Goals must be SMART.

1.  Simple

2.  Measureable

3. Achievable

4. Realistic

5. Timely

Follow this five step method to developing goals for your officiating and they will keep you on track and accelerate your development.

Tommy Moore, retired NFL official, told me that goals are the difference between the official with 10 years experience and the person who is a 3rd year official for the 10th year in a row.

Continuous improvement should be broken down into small steps and begins with a valid and penetrating self-evaluation. Take each game, each week, each season and set goals for your improvement. Tweak your performance constantly, and you will find the end results both rewarding and beneficial to your officiating career.

Finally, write your goals down. Post them where you can see them. These actions will hold you accountable to the goals you set. Include a timeline and review your goals frequently to keep yourself on track. Strive never to repeat a season without some level of improvement.

## Focus Factor #3: Balance

Football officiating can be a very exciting avocation provided you can successfully integrate it into your family and work life. SEC Referee Matt Austin said he didn't believe success in officiating was possible unless your family was supportive. I don't believe balance gets enough attention for its role in officiating. Balancing the demands of family and work with requirements of football officiating can be a daunting task.

James Breeding is an SEC and Big East basketball official who I heard speak recently. James officiated a game in the NCAA tournament that went into 6 overtime periods. He said he walked off the court at 1:37 am and went straight to the hotel room. After two pieces of cold pizza he caught a ride to the LaGuardia Airport to catch a 6 am flight back to Louisville.

When he walked into his office at 9:30 am his boss looked amazed that he was at work. "Didn't I just see you on a basketball court last night?" his boss remarked.

James went on to say that as much as he loved officiating, his primary source of income was at work, his insurance was at work, and his 401K was at work. "I could go down with a blown ACL tomorrow then where would I be?"

I realize that was a basketball story but I felt it truly demonstrated my intent. Continue to assess where officiating football lies within your priorities. Don't let this avocation consume you. Many have fallen victim to a skewed sense of what's important.

## Focus Factor #4: Faith, Family, Vocation

Officiating can get into your blood. I know it's certainly in mine. But putting on the stripes should never get in the way of your faith, family or work.

Ken Rivera, Mountain West Coordinator, tells his officials, "The most important thing that you have, the order of your priorities besides your faith is going to be your family is first, then your employment, and then your officiating, in that order. Once you make your job second and your family third, and football first, you've got it all out of whack. You can't lose sight of that because it's just a game. It's fun and folks that are in officiating are the only ones who know how cool it is, but it's still a game when it comes down to it. And the game's going to go on with or without you."

It is paramount that you consistently analyze where football officiating lies in your priorities. Faith and family must come first. I have seen the damage done to marriages and families when good guys put football ahead of family. Think balance.

I will visit the subject of relationships many times in this text and can't stress enough the value of strong healthy relationships. As you progress in your officiating career, you will not only develop deep and meaningful relationships with your officiating friends; but you will most certainly foster those same qualities with your family, colleagues at work and in the community. Jim Jackson, Ohio Valley Conference Commissioner of Football Officiating; told me officiating gave him over 200 close friends across the country and he valued those friendships more than anything he could ever take away from the game.

Next on your priority list is your job or career. There are some vocations that are better suited to the demands of a busy football official especially as your move up the ladder. My research found multiple educators, lawyers, sales professionals, and law enforcement officers. Jobs with flexible hours and understanding superiors are always a plus. Consider at the Division I or NFL level, all officials must be on site the day before the game. Depending on the length of travel, this stipulation might require you to leave work early to allow sufficient travel time. Multiply that by 12 weeks or longer and you can easily see why having balance in the work place is critical to your future success. More than one aspiring official has been forced to suspend his dreams because the "job got in the way" of his football officiating.

Finally, people get extremely passionate about sports officiating. There isn't anything wrong with that, however, you must work to ensure that officiating does not consume you. If officiating football at the DI or NFL level becomes the most important goal for you, then it spells TROUBLE.

Stories arise each year about people so focused on their schedule, attending the most expensive camps, and who can they talk to about getting into this conference or that conference. Good officials easily become obsessed with their officiating career. Time works against us and the pressure to move up and advance can choke the wind out of people. Soon officiating football becomes the only focus in their lives and it eats away at their core ultimately driving them away from the game they so loved.

I uncovered many tricks and techniques the top level ref's used to stay in touch with their families while traveling. Web cams, video, cell phones were all prevalent. Time management plays a key role during the week with people juggling their family/work roles with film review, rules study and maintaining their physical fitness. Vacations are planned around the downtime between spring scrimmages and the fall season. Several NFL officials told me how they maximized their homeward travel time to get ahead on reviewing their game film. Down time while away at game sites might be spent watching youth football film showcasing the crew member's children. Others planned nights with their spouses during the week and date night with their children (giving Mom a night off as well). Find what works best for your situation, and stick to it. A solid foundation at home makes is so much easier to build a long and rewarding career on the field.

## Focus Factor #5: Fitness & Athletic Ability

If you take nothing else away from this book, please take this tidbit of advice to heart. If you want to advance in the field of football officiating, **you must look and perform like an athlete.**

How you look on and off the field will play a key role in determining how far your officiating career advances.

I posed the same question to all the NCAA conference supervisors and the answer was unanimous. "You are sitting in the stands watching a spring scrimmage and evaluating 5-6 prospective officials. What are 2-3 immediate characteristics you look for in those candidates?"

The answer? You must look like an athlete.

"You better be fit. The more fit you look the faster you're going to move. There's no substitute for looking like an athlete, because you almost have to be an athlete to be an official these days, the way the game's played. It's played quick, everything's done fast. Guys are bigger, faster, stronger, and you've got to be faster, stronger, in better shape than you ever have been. The guys that aren't in shape are not going to be around" said Dick Honig, former Big Ten Referee and current ACC Replay Supervisor.

Now to be frank, football officials have not always been known for their physique or athletic ability. In fact, we can all recall seeing officials in the past on television who were not in the best physical condition. That does not mean necessarily that they were not good officials. There are literally thousands of great rules experts, mechanic gurus, and officials with great judgment out there whose fitness level may be lacking. But the times are changing. Today, all officials must first pass the "eye test.

"You need to be fit and in shape to move around and be athletic, to get yourself in the best position to make the call. Officials spend a lot of time on their physical appearance and conditioning. When the players and coaches see the work that you're doing and the commitment you've made with your body, and see your appearance, it gives you more credibility," said Allen Baynes, NFL Side Judge.

Fitness cannot be stressed enough. Having an athletic look is critically important because you are instantly judged by players and coaches the moment you step on the field. Starting with your general presence, how you stand and walk, how you carry yourself – your physical appearance lends, or removes, credibility and trust. The next factor is even more important in projecting that desired image – how you run.

Now you might be thinking – how I run? How does that play into making it at the top? I suggest that most of us out there have seldom witnessed ourselves running ANYWHERE! I challenge each of you to set up a video camera in the back yard, local high school track or on a field and film yourself running. I personally sought the help of a local track coach to help me improve my run. Some people are just gifted runners. They glide across the field moving effortlessly from place to place. Not me. I pound the ground. I'm built to move things or pick up heavy items. Weight-lifting, no problem, but running... It's a chore.

So I watched myself on video and was very surprised at how I looked. My upper body was very stiff, I didn't have much movement in my arms, and my lower legs didn't bend very much. I looked as if running was very labor-intensive and difficult. Not the image I wanted to project. So I changed it.

I sought the help of a good friend who happens to coach cross country and track at a local high school. Now I'm not saying I am the second coming U'sain Bolt, but what I did was re-engineer how I ran. I worked on the "mechanics" of my run and it has paid great dividends. Not only in the general appearance, but I'm also a better, more efficient runner and that puts me in position to evaluate the action on the field.

Now let me share with you a real world example. I asked Bill Lemmonier, Big Ten referee, about the importance of physical conditioning. Here's what he had to say:

"I can give you this example. Bill Corolla is taking over as supervisor of officials this year in the Big Ten; Dave Perry just retired from that position. But the ratings system that Dave Perry had, every week you were graded, you had judgment was the highest area. I mean, it counted double, your judgment calls. You were also graded on your mechanics, you were graded on the calls you made. In addition, you had an appearance grade which was basically a fitness grade and you could get a score in all these categories from 1 to 7, with 7 being on the high end. Well, from being around the league enough I knew that every week, to get a 7 in every category, well…nobody got 7's. A high score in any category was a 6."

"I worked 11 games and if I walk out on that field and I get a 5 or a 6 from the rater in my appearance, and it's because I keep the gut off, because I come out there looking athletic or my movement's fluid. I come out there and get a 5 or a 6 every week and another referee, who's also a pretty good darn referee, but he's just out of shape, he goes out there and he gets a 3 or a 4 every week for his appearance. Well he just gave up 2 to 3 points a week to me for the final ratings, and the ratings are what are going to determine your bowl status. So if we worked 11 games and I'm 33 points ahead of you just on my appearance, I could kick 3 or 4 judgment calls more than you and still come out with a better score at the end of the year."

Yet another critical aspect of fitness is being prepared for the level of play as you rise in the ranks. Mike Cary describes it best, "The level of play from high school to junior college takes a pretty good step. The athleticism is higher, the intensity is higher, and there is more at stake. Then from junior college to the Division I level everything takes another good leap forward. The professionalism, the organization, coaching, speed, size, talent is all more congealed as a professional presentation. But I don't think anything prepares you for making the transition from college to the NFL. It's like skipping from Pop Warner to Division I."

Don Lucas, Sunbelt Coordinator, believes simply won't see out-of-shape officials rising to the next level any more. Physically fit football officials are here to stay and I hope I've communicated the importance of staying in top shape. Your officiating career will depend on it.

## Focus Factor #6: Look the Part

Perception and believability are brothers to fitness and athletic ability. As an aspiring official seeking to advance, we look for every angle to give us a leg up. You must have field presence. You must be able to command respect. Opinions are formed in an instant but they follow you for a very long time.

Now what does that mean? Presence is an air of confidence that you demonstrate on the field. It's not arrogance or cockiness, but you exude an image of self-assurance so that coaches and players around you feel you have the ability to officiate this game. Having confidence in your ability will improve not only your self-perception but also how you are perceived by the players and coaches. Consequently, there will be a higher level of believability to your calls.

I also suggest you get a friend or spouse to attend one of your games and film YOU. Don't film the play, film the official. Game film tends to be focused on the play and often times the officials are not in the picture. Game film can be good for evaluating fouls and situations but it is often lacking when used to improve mechanics and general image.

Look at yourself during dead ball periods, time-outs, and changes in possession. Look at how you move from one spot to another. Do you move with a purpose? How do you stand? Do you slouch? What is your body language? All these are important to projecting an image that will not only get you noticed but also lend credibility to your game.

Finally, here is a tip that will help set you apart from about half of all football officials on the field. Billy Alton, WVIAC Supervisor, has a mantra he tells all of his officials, "why walk when you can run." He is 100% correct. Walking looks lazy and projects a lack of seriousness. Always hustle. Move with a purpose. It will instantly impact your presence in a visible and positive manner.

I believe that if all other characteristics are equal: rules knowledge, mechanics, judgment, experience, between two officials competing for the same job; the official who looks best in his uniform wins. Take your conditioning, fitness level and physical appearance seriously. Make sure you pass "the eye test."

**Focus Factor #7: Self Discipline/Time Management**

The best officials also happen to be extremely disciplined. We don't have coaches to encourage us; we rely on ourselves to remain engaged and motivated. I have always believed that football officiating wasn't about getting a thousand things right but it was about getting ten things right one thousand times. If you use self-discipline to approach your game day in, day out; you develop a consistency that will help you when the time comes to move to the next level. The habits we form at the early stages in our career become the foundation on which NCAA and NFL careers are built. Lack of self-discipline will ultimately lead to complacency and stop your advancement in its tracks.

John McGrath, NFL Head Linesman; believes desire and self-discipline can give him a competitive advantage. "If you want to be better you have to have the desire to be the best. I can remember my son many a times looking at me during the wintertime. I'd be down in the basement lifting weights or I'd go jogging in the snow, and he'd ask me "What are you going out jogging for?" I remember one time he asked me "What are you going out jogging for? It's -10°!" I'd always tell him "Bradley – there's a whole bunch of people who want to get into the National Football League. How many of them do you think are out here jogging in -10°? I'm going to do whatever it takes for me to get to the top." That is a perfect definition of self-discipline.

All officials, regardless of level, need to possess excellent time management skills. The combination of work, family, career and officiating can amount to a hectic schedule. As I spoke with top level football officials, it became apparent that time management was a critical skill that made a difference in each official's career. The demands on their time as they climbed the ladder do not diminish. You may have heard teachers and professors say that for every hour of class, you must spend 4-5 hours in preparation. The same can be said of a top football official. Countless hours of

43

preparation culminate in three hours of football in which we strongly believe we are successful only when we are not noticed! There is a ton of hard work and very little glory.

The better you manage your time early in your career, the easier the transition will become when you advance. I found the higher level you achieve on the officiating career ladder, the amount of preparation is inversely proportional to the number of minutes on the field. The demands on your time and schedule don't get any easier as you move up.

This rang true with me in my first year at the college level. Game film was available for downloading on Sunday night. Monday night, in addition to a JV high school game, was also video review night. Factor in daily rules study and you can see how time management and preparation go hand in hand. There were more than a few video review sessions that occurred at midnight!

## Focus Factor #8: Character/Be A Team Player?

*No man is an island.*

I wrote earlier that conference supervisors had two common requirements when evaluating prospective officials. One was appearance. You must look and move like an athlete. The second common characteristic isn't quite as obvious. They want good people. Now that's a pretty broad term so let me attempt to define it. There are many officials that have a great look, run well, make great calls, know the rules; but fail miserably when it comes to dealing effectively with people.

I heard this stated in countless ways but the underlying theme was the same. You must be a good person to advance and this becomes so critical at the higher levels that its absence can prevent you from moving up and grind your career to a screeching halt. "You just can't have any character flaws. If you do it will come back to haunt you and keep you from moving up," said Don Lucas, Sunbelt Conference. Trust me when I say that intangibles such as character and integrity are as vitally important as rules knowledge and mechanics the higher you progress on the ladder of success.

Mike Carey, NFL referee and Super Bowl veteran believes one of the biggest improvements officiating has brought him is in terms of character development. Possessing the ability to look inside and be honest with yourself about what you did on a particular play. Honestly assessing your performance is a very important part of this game and is a key element in becoming a good football official.

You must be adept at dealing with conflict, handling emotions, communicating with coaches, players and other officials. You must be able to keep your emotions in check in times where the situation may be erupting around you. Realize that you are on display at every game, in every locker room, at every association meeting. Coaches will call you by first name. Fellow officials will smile (or cringe) when they see your name on their schedule.

Your personal character is on trial and believe me when I say…people are taking notice. So you might be thinking, 'How would a Doug Rhoads or a Rogers Redding ascertain my interpersonal skills?' They pick up the phone and make a few well-placed calls and you become the subject of a very informal but effective "background check."

I'll simply summarize this topic by saying that the highest praise a football official can receive is for a fellow official to state, "I'll share the field with you any time." As you improve and advance, your reputation becomes more and more public, on and off the field. It takes more than skill and talent to reach the NCAA Division I and NFL levels. Conflict resolution, communication, honesty and integrity are the distinguishing factors and it is never too soon to begin working on them.

### Focus Factor #9: External Affirmation

*Who Will Pat My Back?*

If you are going to become a successful football official, you must be able to deal with a lack of praise or affirmation. Over the years you most likely have received attention and positive reinforcement from parents and family. In school the feedback came from your teachers, coaches and friends.

Then you enter into football officiating. Your first game, you caught a great hold on a tackle. It was a take-down at the point of attack and you saw it plain as day. Great call and you nailed it. Did you hear anyone in the stands cheering for you? Were the cheerleaders chanting your name or cannons booming in the end zone? Did the coaches pat you on the back for a job well-done?

Reality is this: Positive affirmation is not readily available in sports officiating.

If you are seeking your name in lights, or articles written about you in the news, you might need to reconsider. Your positive feedback comes from within. In time you will learn to become your own worst critic…and biggest ally. Just don't expect to get any love from the players, coaches or fans!

## Focus Factor #10: Athletic IQ

*Do You Have Football Smarts?*

You may have heard people remark that someone has "a great feel for the game." They are referring to a person's athletic IQ. Let's define that.

Doug Rhoads, Don Lucas, Rogers Redding, Gerald Austin, Ken Rivera…they all mentioned it in one form or another. Top level prospects need to understand the game of football.

Athletic IQ doesn't require a person to be an all state football player or a college phenomenon. You don't need an advanced degree or twenty years of experience. It means that you have an understanding for competitive athletics and team sports. It is quite possible that you may never have participated in a team sport.

You understand the emotions that are involved in the game and the jubilation that comes with winning and the anguish that accompanies losing. You realize how important practice is, what a role preparation takes, what it means to be a good teammate. Bottom line: you understand what it takes to be a winner.

We need to understand these same things to be a successful official. On the field, you are tasked with managing the game. Emotions are constantly present: yours, the players and the coaches. Understanding the importance of emotion in the game of football will undoubtedly help you handle the many situations you will encounter on the field.

Are you a student of the game? When you watch football, do you look at the game through the eyes of the players, coaches or officials? You probably know people who can name the players, quote their stats, and state the team rankings. These people are students of the game. Now I should clarify one thing. There is a difference between a student of the game and a fan. Top level officials study the game in order to become better at anticipating and properly responding to the situation at hand. They study ALL sports to better understand how people react in competitive environments. These officials attempt to learn from every play, every call, and every game regardless of the teams competing. Learning never stops regardless of the level you reach.

## Focus Factor #11: Success Leaves Traces

One fact I found prevalent in the officials I interviewed for this book was they were all successful off the field. Whether in their professional careers, with their spouses and children, in their community; all had experienced success in not only football, but in life. They each possessed a tremendous level of self-confidence which comes in handy in this humbling past-time. Integrity, judgment, dedication, perseverance are just a few expressive words used to describe the people behind the stripes.

You see, I believe a pattern of success can become a self-fulfilling prophecy. If you examined the resumes of the top NFL and NCAA officials you would find consistent and demonstrated success, both on and off the field. Past can be a great predictor of the future. *Success leaves traces.*

# *Zebra Tales*

Allen Baynes, NFL Side Judge

*There's always funny moments that happen, and that's actually how we keep a little bit of the sanity in this tough, pressure packed job we have, because it can get a little intense. Folks can get mad at you, but the funny stories we have with each other out on the field are really what keep us sane. It's really what makes it fun.*

*I was working the Cincinnati / Louisville game several years back. It was at Louisville and our head linesman has a tight ruling on a scoring play. It's a touchdown, the guy dives over the middle, stretches the ball forward and he rules it a touchdown for Cincinnati. The Louisville people weren't real happy with him. As a result, he got hit with a chicken bone, a fried chicken leg, and he got hit right in the head with a chicken bone. So he came to me and goes, "Allen, I guess somebody didn't agree with me. They didn't like that call so much that they threw their chicken leg and hit me in the head with it." We just got the biggest kick out of it.*

*That was one thing that we never thought we'd get hit with at football games would be a chicken bone. Stuff like that, I couldn't make that up. It's intense and things are going crazy but what people don't understand is that we're sitting down on the field, not visibly laughing out loud, but to ourselves we're just cracking up at the fact that we're sitting there getting ridiculed. Sixty thousand people are mad and screaming at us and one person decides to throw a chicken bone. That was the one thing thinking back that I'll always remember; I'll always get a kick out of that.*

# Chapter 3

## Get in the Game

◆━━━━━━━━━━━━━━━━━━━━━━━━━━━━━━━◆

*"In the fog of war, that's when we stand out." - Jeff Triplette, NFL Referee*

L et's take a close look at what happens at the very beginning of a football official's prospective career. Let's assume for the moment that you have never officiated a game of football in your life. Where do you begin?

Why football? There are several motivational factors at work here. Most common, is a love of football. You might have a friend or a family member that officiates and have discussed how to get involved with that person. Some associations advertise the need for new officials in print, radio and television venues. At the very basic level, you are simply interested in the donning the zebra stripes.

Let me be clear here...there is a growing need in every state, every community, and every youth league for football officials. The enrollment in youth sports continues to rise and the number of officials continue to decline (in all sports, not just football) so there is now, and will continue to be, a need for officials.

## 1. Gather Information

The first step is to gather information on local football officiating opportunities. Some of this can be accomplished via the Internet. You can search the web for youth leagues and local officials associations. Many of these groups maintain informative websites which will provide contact information with the leaders of those groups.

Call your local high school athletic department. Speak with the athletic director or head football coach. They will certainly be happy to inform you of key members in the officiating community whom you may contact for more information.

I would also suggest that you reach out to your state's high school athletics association. You can access this information at www.nhfs.org. If you have trouble finding a local association or officiating resource, contact your state's athletic office and they most certainly can point you in the right direction.

## 2. Exposure

The second step, and most often overlooked, is to get a good look at what officials do. Find a local official and ask to ride along with them to a game or association meeting. Don't think you have to talk to a Big East or NFL referee in order to get a behind-the-scenes look at officiating. There are thousands of great officials at the high school level who have a passion for officiating. I guarantee you can find a willing person to discuss you intentions, gain exposure to officiating and help you get started on the right path. You just have to ask.

Attend a local youth league or high school football game. Make a point to meet the officials at half-time or between games on a Saturday afternoon. You will find this group warm and inviting, eager to talk to anyone interested in officiating football.

Call the coaches and administrators of youth leagues, recreational leagues, children's leagues. Visit your local YMCA. Ask who assigns the officials for their games. You will find the right people who can get you started.

## 3. Ride Along

Once you've identified a local resource, take the next step and ask to ride along with them to a game. You can't fully appreciate football officiating from watching college or professional football on television. A fan's view isn't sufficient when evaluating whether you'd like to become a football official. Spend a few hours on a

Friday night and experience what happens at a varsity contest from the eyes of an official. You will view officiating from a different perspective, rest assured.

Listen to the band play, the fans cheer (or complain!), the press box announcer, the coaches and players interact; *experience* the true essence of a football game. You most likely could attend a Saturday youth league game and stand behind a wing (sideline) official during the game and ask questions between plays. Talk about perspective!

## 4. Officiate – Yes or No?

Now you might think that going to all this trouble just to get started officiating football won't be worth the effort. My reply is: Football officiating is not for everyone. It is a demanding avocation and the decision to become a football official should not be taken lightly. The game requires football officials to be dedicated, prepared and reliable. Officiating requires thick skin and humility. You must be willing to learn the game of football from the eyes of the official, not the fan. What you see on Sunday with your favorite NFL team will seldom apply on your Sunday youth league game.

Having said that, the rewards of becoming a member of the officiating community are immense and well worth the effort. I've often used the word "fraternity" when describing my association. The camaraderie and fellowship which results when people come together combining the love of football and a passion for officiating cannot be adequately described in a few words. You just have to experience it from the inside.

Associations lose a large percentage of their rookie officials each year because I believe the recruits don't have a good idea of what football officiating requires. I think retention could be improved if the candidates spent a bit more time on the front end understanding exactly what's required.

So you think you are ready to take the plunge? Does officiating the game of football sound appealing? Ask yourself these questions first:

- Will my family commitments allow me the opportunity to spend time each week away from them in order to officiate football games? I intentionally placed this in the top spot. Having your family buy-in is critical to long-term success in football officiating.

- Will my career offer the ability to leave work with sufficient time to arrive at games by the scheduled start time? Freshman, JV and Varsity games often begin as early as 5 pm. Will your employer be flexible with you in regards to honoring game times?

- Am I willing to dedicate sufficient time to learning the rules, mechanics, attend association meetings, training, etc?

- Officiating football can be physically rigorous and fitness level is important for multiple reasons. Are you willing to maintain the level of fitness necessary to officiate football?

If you answered YES to the above questions, you are well on your way to a successful football officiating career!

## 5. Join a Local Association

This step is not a requirement however; I strongly believe all officials should belong to their local association. You may find you can officiate your area youth or intramural leagues without joining a local or state association. I would not let the absence of a local officials association stop me from calling games if there is opportunity for you to work in those leagues. Take every available chance to get snaps and experience.

If such an organization exists in your local area, I can't stress how important the association is for a new official and the support which comes along with it. Some organizations have training classes for first year officials. Others have less formal methods. Some use OJT or FJA. OJT is On-The-Job training and FJA is Follow-Joe-Around. Both examples are very common in most training plans and you can expect at minimum, some experience and training via these methods. All associations, regardless of size and scope, will be able to put you in touch with the right people that can give you the proper start and get you out on the football field.

These groups typically meet on a weekly basis during the season and less often (or not at all) during the off-season. You will find belonging to a football official's organization will offer you the chance to meet others with similar interests, find new friends, even the potential for professional networking. But most importantly, the local association will provide you access to more seasoned officials who can help you develop, improve and move up.

Recruiting of new prospects typically beings in the spring although, some larger associations recruit new members year around. New official training can begin as early as July in advance of the regular football season and continues through your first season. High school football is a fall sport and seasons commonly run August to November. (Check your state's athletic association for more information.) While it varies among associations, training should prepare you to officiate at the beginning levels in 4-6 weeks and you build on that experience through the season.

My research interviewing NCAA and NFL officials revealed that EVERY top level official got their start in the same manner as I've described above. Not one NFL official skipped over Pee Wee football. The stories have different twists and turns, but the general path was always the same. The foundation for a rewarding career in football officiating begins in your hometown, at your local high school, with local players and coaches. How far we ultimately rise in this avocation is based on many factors; but where we start is, in the simplest terms, the same place. The branches of the tree grow in different directions, but they all have the same roots.

So you have decided to don the stripes and hit the field. You joined your local association. You are excited about what your first season will bring. The next step is crucial to your long-term development, advancement and enjoyment as a football official. What you need now is someone to show you the ropes, be your sounding board, your Go-To guy. You need a Mentor.

# *Zebra Tales*

◆━━━━━━━━━━━━━━━━━━━━━━━━━━━━━━━━◆

Vic Winnek, Great West Umpire

*This is a funny story; I got home from work on a Thursday and had 2 congratulatory voicemail messages left for me. I then received a call from another official congratulating me on getting in to the WCFOA (Div. 1-AA Independent; now part of the Great West Conference – Cal Poly San Luis Obispo, UC Davis, Southern Utah University). I was told letters had been mailed and all the new hires had received theirs. I had not received a letter or telephone call from the supervisor. Knowing that letters of hire required the new hire to reply within three days, I waited two days with angst before making a phone to the supervisor. I called three times before deciding to leave a message. The message left was something like this:*

*"Mr. Wilson, this is Vic Winnek. This is a rather unusually situation I am calling about. I have received a few telephone calls form officials on your staff indicating that you may have hired me, but I have not received any correspondence from you. I understand you need a response by today and I am calling to let you know that if you did send me a letter of hire I did not receive it but am totally honored and whole heartedly accept any position. But if I am mistaken and you did not send me a letter, this is the most embarrassing telephone call I have ever made and I am so sorry to disturb you and apologize for this rather forward telephone message and hope you will forget I even made this call. But if you do need an official I am very excited to work for you..."*

*I hung up the phone and spent the next few hours wishing I had not left that message and figured I had just ended my officiating career.*

*Around 9 O'clock that night Don Wilson called, laughing and realizing how awkward it was for me to leave such a message, he eased my fears and said that he had sent me a letter but it must still be in the mail and asked me to join his group. I was on cloud nine, practically standing at attention in a cold sweat as! He was wonderful; I still smile when I think of that call.*

# Chapter 4
## The Barrel of Monkeys

*"I'm a firm believer in that we can't do this by ourselves."*
- Bill LeMonnier, Big 10 Referee

T here were a few common themes present in every top level official's career I examined. One was presence of mentors at each and every stage of development over each referee's career. Credit was given to many for getting them into the sport. Other's paid tribute to those that helped open doors to advance or provided deep and meaningful coaching and education along the way. Collectively they stressed the importance of having a mentor and most still relied on mentors regardless of what level they had achieved.

A mentor is defined as a wise and trusted advisor and every official should have one when they begin officiating. A mentor can help a new official, both on and off the field. Starting out in your rookie year can be a daunting task. A mentor can teach, monitor and encourage a new official especially when obstacles present themselves and the new official might entertain giving the avocation up. It is commonly felt that turnover in the officiating ranks could be dramatically reduced if every newly minted official took part in a comprehensive mentoring program.

Some associations have complete plans in place to provide the framework for mentoring to occur. It may be a requirement and the mentors are assigned very early in a rookie's season. Other times the process is much less formal. Officials are left on their own to identify approach and convince a mentor to take them under the wing. The further you climb up the ladder, the more often it seems that finding the right mentor lies squarely on the aspiring official's shoulders. No matter how you obtain a mentor, their input and guidance is critical in your development. Don't let the absence of a mentoring program stop you from finding one.

In the perfect world, a new official is matched up with a veteran official who becomes the new referee's point of contact the first or second year. Having a person to ease the stress of learning an entirely new skill, keeping you positive and moving in the right direction, and just someone you can call to talk over game situations, rules questions and mechanics could positively affect a decision to return for the next season. NFL Umpire Tony Michalek spoke in great detail about how important it is for the mentor to be involved and want to be a part of developing the new official. "You have to call them up and talk to them. You have to make the time to go watch them work. That will mean the world to them and you have to bring them along slowly," said Michalek.

As you advance, you should pay close attention to the process of selecting a mentor. Ken Rivera, Mountain West Coordinator, suggests identifying candidates that are working at the level which you aspire, humbly approaching them and ask for their help. Let them know you have ambitions of reaching their level. Ask what made them successful and then ask for advice on how to improve your individual game.

Don't be discouraged if the person declines your offer. It happens. He may not have the time to invest in you. Thank them kindly and be appreciative of their honesty. Better to focus your efforts with a mentor that can be engaged and supportive.

Tony Michalek gives this advice, "They'll tell you, 'Hey, if you've got any questions don't be afraid to call.' Well then don't be afraid to call. How many times do people say, 'If you need anything, give me a call' and nobody calls? Don't be afraid to make the phone call. Don't be afraid to come up to a meeting and say, 'Listen - this happened in my game the other night. How should I handle this? I wasn't sure and this is what I did.' Don't be afraid. Officials love to talk about officiating."

You might think the mentoring ceases to exist at the highest levels but in fact, it may actually be MORE important. Allen Baynes, a NFL Side Judge, told a great story which we can all take away a gem of advice. Each NFL crew position has a position coach who is a former NFL officials still involved in teaching and training as a part of his current responsibilities. During Allen's preseason games, his position coach actually spent time on the field with him and offered the opportunity to ask questions, talk about mechanics and positioning and giving Allen immediate feedback.

Allen stated that during the preseason clinic, position coaching intended for the newer officials, was offered to anyone that was interested. It involves weekly calls, film review and general coaching. Once offered, the response from the veterans was overwhelming. Even guys that had officiated Super Bowls were requesting the assistance. "That made a big impression on me, that it doesn't matter what level you're at, how many years you got at that level, you still need to try to get better at what you're doing," said Baynes.

Mentoring at the top is comprised more of constructive criticism than of praise. Several officials remarked that the number of calls offering congratulations was far out-weighted by the calls to discuss how to improve your play-calling, positioning or mechanics. Mentoring occurs at all levels regardless of what heights you achieve. Here is how Bill LeMonnier, Big Ten Referee, feels about mentoring.

"Jerry Markbreit helped me on several occasions. I've been to Jerry Markbreit's house and sat with him for five hours at a time, just to be more proficient at speaking on a microphone and giving signals. From the first time I refereed I got so many nice compliments back, nobody said anything about the calls I made but they liked the way I handled the microphone. They liked the way I did announcements; they liked the flow of the game. There was a good tempo; the communication with the coaches was good. So again, I think I'm pretty competent at what I do with my calls but it isn't what separates me from the other people. It's a people business and I think no matter what position you work out there, if you've got good people skills, dealing with the players cause it's an emotional game, dealing with the coaches who obviously get emotional, they might not walk away agreeing with you but you're able to diffuse situations. I think that's a skill that can be taught and worked on but I think the people who either have natural talent with it or who have taken it to another level. That's what's helped them with their success."

Being a mentor isn't just about patting someone on the back and being their pal. Sometimes it takes guts and a willingness to put aside formalities in order to really help your protégé improve.

LeMonnier continues, "I had guys that would flat out look you in the eye and they'd tell you when you did something positive, and they'd flat out tell you when you needed to change something. They did it without being judgmental. But they could look you in the eye and they could say "Hey, here's what I would recommend you to do if that situation happens again." That's what you need from people. It's great to have somebody pat you on the back but that's not going to help you improve. If it needs to change, somebody's got to look you in the eye and tell you. You have to be able to accept that and move on."

Now I can't take credit for this story. I heard it first from J.T. Orr, an NBA and NCAA basketball referee; but I do like the story and the message it delivers. Do you remember as a kid (or parent) that game called **Barrel of Monkeys**? There was a plastic barrel which contained 10 or 15 plastic monkeys. Each of the monkeys had a hand that stretched out above their head and one that stretched below them. The hands were formed like hooks. Remember that?

The object of the game was to see how many monkeys you could pick up out of the barrel basically creating a chain of monkeys hooked at their hands. You were only allowed to touch one monkey. As one monkey came out of the barrel, he reaches back down to grab another monkey and pulls him up.

As I examined the careers of successful officials I began to see a pattern emerge. Officials have mentors above them always pulling them upwards, helping them work to be better officials, learning from the veterans above them. Every NFL or NCAA football official we've interviewed spoke about two or three key people in their careers that mentored them as they were coming up the ranks.

Jim Jackson, a former referee from the Sunbelt Conference and currently the Ohio Valley Coordinator of Football Officiating feels strongly about mentors. "I think anybody who's had any measure of success in this business; they've had somebody who took more than a casual interest in them as a person and them as an official."

That's basically the monkey reaching back down in the barrel and pulling up another monkey. Comical sure, but it's a good analogy.

That's only the half of it. The fraternity of football officiating appears to hold fast to an understood tradition that the successful officials continue to reach down and become mentors. So that means that the young or new aspiring officials need to be aware of the importance of mentoring from the bottom up. It's not an automatic process, one that just happens without effort. As a new official, you must humble seek your mentor in order to establish this important relationship. That's being the monkey *in the barrel.*

Mentors can provide numerous benefits, regardless if you are reaching up or down. Whether it be rules study groups, learning mechanics, or modeling yourself after someone that is at the level you wish to be...mentoring is vital to reaching your goals and can often reduce the time it takes to achieve them. Learning occurs from both perspectives and mentors often remark they got more out of the relationship they felt, than did the officials they mentored.

Either way, mentoring is a key fundamental concept on any football official's path to success. Proper attention should be devoted to the identification and cultivation of those mentoring relationships.

Just ask Ken Rivera, former Mountain West referee and current MWC Coordinator of Football Officiating. "I think mentoring is the absolute most important strategy that an official can have. If they want to advance or even get better at their current level; they need to find that person who's working at the top in all those high school games and gets all the playoffs. Humble yourself and go to that person and say, "Hey, I want to be where you are. What are some things that you've done to make you successful to get there and, knowing my personality traits, my officiating style, what are some things that I can do to improve myself?" That's at every level."

Finally, NFL Referee Mike Carey puts yet another spin on mentoring, "I believe we all mentor each other. It happens at every level and between any two people who communicate with each other. There are those who are extraordinary, but I believe it happens on a peer level as well as an experienced-to-inexperienced level. That's one of the strong points about officiating...everyone is there to help out."

As you can see, the presence of mentors along your officiating career path is vitally important. But even more essential is to take the advice, coaching and constructive criticism and put that information in your improvement plans. Involve your mentors in your goal-setting, make them aware of your aspirations and celebrate your successes. You will strengthen and enhance the relationship and the resulting dividends will far outweigh your investment.

# *Zebra Tales*

Doug Rhoads, ACC Coordinator of Football Officials

*Well, I mean there's literally dozens of anecdotal things that deal with situations on the field where coaches say something, you say something back, or you know whatever happens there. I frankly don't like to focus so much on plays that have occurred, because once again I think the job of the official is to go out there, do your thing and leave, and nobody knows you were there. I've conducted extensive investigative work over the last 30 years and I haven't found anybody yet that paid for a ticket to go watch the officials.*

*So as a result, get in and get out, do your thing and you're fine. This goes back to my high school days. I was working a state high school playoff game in Virginia and at that time, I can't remember who the competing teams were, but it appeared as if a guy ran on the field late and was the 12th player, and the coach is going nuts. I had counted and I know they only had 10 to start with, so that was the 11th player that came on. They were legal and I don't flag it. Well after the play, the coach calls time out and goes cuckoo, "I can't believe it. I just talked to my guy upstairs; he says that that was the 12th guy, how come you didn't throw the flag?" I said, "Coach, they only had ten and that was the 11th player that was legal." "I can't believe it…" and going on and on.*

*Finally, the time out's up and I'm getting tired of talking to him and getting ready to go back out, and he says, "Well, I'm telling you were wrong." I said, "Well, I'm telling you, you weren't right." I said, "I'll bet you twenty bucks when you look at that film, you count it and you'll see." He says,*

*"You're on," so we leave. Well, the guy who assigned our high school games was an old time ACC referee, ran a sporting goods store in Charlottesville, and he called me on about Thursday of that week following it. I had forgotten all about it and went on, and I don't remember all that happened. He said "I've got an envelope that came here to the sporting goods store addressed to you."*

*So I go down there later in the day and pick the envelope up. It had a $20 bill in it, it was from the coach. It read, "Doug: You were right, I was wrong. Have a great year." And he signed it. I'll never forget that. I had completely forgotten about, that I had said "I'll bet you". I thought that was funny. He conceded.*

# Chapter 5
## #1 Tool for Success

◆────────────────────────────────────────◆

*"When you see yourself on tape the tape doesn't lie."*
- Ken Rivera, Mountain West Coordinator

I mentioned in an earlier chapter there were two common themes present in each top-level football official I interviewed. The first was the impact of mentors in their careers. The second is the importance of video and its use towards continuous improvement of their officiating skills.

Video is the single greatest tool in your toolbox. Breaking down your video is the equivalent to officiating three games for every game you actually work. It accelerates your learning curve and puts your improvement path on fast forward.

The fact that it's so valuable yet so little used should be the only reason you need. If you are looking for ways to set yourself apart from your competition, here it is. This is your single most important differentiating factor. It can truly revolutionize your game.

There are two basic types of video review.

1. Your game film

2. Any game film

I point out the differences for a reason. Reviewing your film will skyrocket *your* development. It has a direct impact on you as an official. It immediately shows your strong points, but at the same time shows you what you need to work on. As Ken Rivera said, the film doesn't lie.

Watching other game film is good for a completely different reason. Football officiating experiences can be measured in several ways. One in particular which applies here is *number of snaps*. There simply is no substitute for getting live snaps. Dick Honig, former Big Ten referee and owner of Honig's Whistle Stop, pointed out to me that reviewing film, *any film*, is as close to live snaps as you can get.

NFL Referee Mike Carey said when he was first hired into the NFL, they gave him a tape of the calls a top NFL official (who worked the same position) had the year before. He took the tape and watched it over and over again and he still couldn't see what was called. He watched hours and hours of tape in the beginning trying to get better and because there was a foul called and I couldn't find it on tape. Carey said, "That was a great learning experience. When I first entered the NFL, I wasn't sure if I was going to make it. If I couldn't see the calls on tape and at a slower speed, how was I going to be able to make that call at full speed? But after watching it over and over, you ingrain those actions in your head and it becomes part of your mental muscle memory. I'm known for knowing the rules, but I spend much more time on film than on rules."

So video review of your games and of games in general, are two aspects of this critical process in the advancement of your skills. Let's take a closer look at this important tool.

## Your Game Film

Supervisors and commissioners agree that you can accelerate your development by a factor of four by just watching half of your games and breaking down the video. Let me put that in different terms for you. You can pack four seasons into one season just by diligently obtaining and reviewing your game film.

This is precisely the reason it can set you apart from your competition. Few officials have the discipline to make this step a part of development plan on a consistent basis. At the DI level, it's a given but not so much at the lower levels.

I'll bet you can think of literally hundreds of reasons why you cannot obtain your film or find the time to review it. Let's reverse that thought process. What are some excuses to *find* the time? Here is one that comes to mind: Game fees at the NCAA Division I level are what most high school officials make in half their season. If you possessed a tool that could get you to the top four times faster, would you use it? If officiating football at the DI level is your goal, then I can guarantee video review is a prerequisite.

Video review is great because in the comfort of your home, it strips away the emotion and hype of the game and lets you analyze the different components of your performance. Over the course of a season, you can identify areas where you need improvement and chart your progress game to game. Video is a humbling tool and you must be completely honest with what you see.

Your crew could break down your game film together. You could get your mentor to watch some video with you. Realizing your video review skills might be in need of some improvement, your mentor can help you with the nuances and intricacies of film review. You could do a pre-assessment of your game and then see if your mentor agrees with your evaluation. Over time, your review skills will improve and so will your performance.

## Obtaining the Video

There are a number of ways to get film from your games. According to Allen Baynes, NFL Side Judge, "I'd call the school beforehand and tell the coach or athletic director that I want a copy of the film. I would take a FedEx box and put a blank tape in there and go ahead and pay for the postage, so the school's not paying for anything. They've just got to simply take the time to record a copy of the tape and just drop it in the mail to my house. The schools understood why I wanted to do it; they watched film and I told them I wanted to watch film to get better, so they appreciated that."

Ken Rivera suggested including a $5 bill for the film tech at the school. Just a little something to help out.

This year I took their advice and purchases blank DVDs, mailers and postage. I self-addressed and stamped 10 mailers and put a blank DVD in each one. Postage was $1.60 for each mailer and the total cost of all materials totaled approximately $50. The Wednesday before each game I would send an email to the Athletic Director at the home school with a short message stating that I was hoping to obtain a copy of the game film. I would specifically state that our local association was trying to improve the quality of officiating and that game film was an important tool for that to occur. Everyone can appreciate officials trying to improve. We were typically met at the school by a staffer and I'd provide the blank DVD and mailer to them asking that it get in the film person's hands. As a result I was successful in 7 of 10 attempts and while I didn't follow-up with the three missing DVD's, I'm certain I could have obtained those as well with a phone call and a little effort.

In my college conference, all game film is uploaded to a service called Game Tape Exchange (you can listen to an in-depth interview with Chris Cobley, the founder of Game Tape Exchange by visiting www.profootballreferee.com). Usually by Sunday evening, the game film was available for download in both sideline and end zone views. My crews also used film review as a component of each Saturday's pre-game routine. This upcoming season the crew is planning a weekly conference call to review the game film in depth prior to the pre-game meeting.

**Breaking Down Tape**

I spent 2-3 hours on Monday and Tuesday of each week reviewing game film from both my college games and the DVD's from the high schools. During every game, I'd make notes on my game card of specific plays, penalties or situations I'd like to review. At the NCAA level, the conference supervisor or technical advisor present at each game would debrief the crews and I'd take notes on specific call-outs to review. It's also important to note that you can benefit from ANY situations, not just plays where you were involved. There was numerous times where the three deep officials (I worked the field judge or side judge position) on my college crew would discuss and debate certain calls in order to determine their validity, accuracy or importance. Almost weekly there were phone calls amongst officials discussing certain plays we'd reviewed on film. Learn from every play situation the video provides, not just where you are the focal point.

Jim Jackson, OVC Coordinator, says it best:

*The number one thing that is paramount in game preparation is film study. Today we have access to film nearly instantly. We can download videos on Sunday from games on Saturday. We had that available to us in the Sunbelt for the last three years I was there. So on Sunday I was able to get the film from Saturday's game. We had a foul report so I was able to view every play, review every foul and it was my intention, and I did this every week, I took the video and rather than looking at the whole game, because there's only thirty or forty plays in a football game that matter, if that many. You just don't know which ones those are until they've already passed. So what I did was edit the video so that I had every foul. Every time we threw a flag you were going to see that on Friday night from the game on Saturday.*

*In addition I would have every play that the coordinator may have mentioned, every play that an observer may have mentioned, and every play that a coach may have questioned. In addition any play that any member of the crew might have a question about that night. So I will have a list, chronologically, before we start editing film of all of those plays. I would then prepare that film of those highlights, as well as make a copy of the entire game for every member of the crew. So I did a lot of work with film. On Friday night when we got there, we'd look at those thirty plays, they last a minute and a half a piece or so, so in forty minutes we'd review every play in the game that mattered. I learned that because if you go there with a full game tape and instantly begin looking for something to happen at 2:58 in the first, that takes some time and you lose your effectiveness. So what I attempted to do was be very, very efficient in film preparation and film review so we got the most of it during the game weekend. Film review is one of those big things you do each week to get ready for the next game.*

I'm confident that breaking down my tape improved my mechanics, my play-calling and my overall game. I also believe that if I want to advance, film review will become a standard operating practice each week so my exposure to film early in my career can better prepare me for what might lie ahead.

SEC Referee Matt Austin believes film can enhance one of the key attributes of a successful official. "You can teach and improve judgment with coaching and plenty of film work."

It's such a powerful tool fully utilized at the highest levels that I'm still amazed at how little it's used in the development and advancement of aspiring officials particularly at the lower levels. Simply put, there is no faster way to accelerate your learning and improvement that by properly reviewing your performance on film.

## *Zebra Tales*

◆━━━━━━━━━━━━━━━━━━━━━━━━━━━━━━◆

Ken Rivera, Mountain West Coordinator of Football Officiating

*When I speak to officiating groups I always talk about this story because it involves my friend Bill Leavy back in 1987, when we were working on an officiating crew together down in New Mexico, at New Mexico State. It was our third year in; we both got in around 1984 and I was the head linesman. In those days we worked a six man mechanic and we had a game down in New Mexico, where near the end of a game, this quarterback for this one team runs to my sideline. He gets hit and fumbles... It's like a three point game real late in the game and the coach from the losing team was on the hot seat that year, because he wasn't doing very well at winning games.*

*I had blown an inadvertent whistle. The defense recovers and the defense is up by four points late in the game. So the defense recovers right on my sideline and I blow an inadvertent whistle, my third year in. One of my mentors was referee, Larry Rice, and of course my other mentor, who I have all the time, is Bill Leavy, he's the side judge across the other side of the field. Again, we worked six men during those days. So I blow the whistle, and everybody hears it. They start pointing at me, "He blew the whistle! He blew the whistle!"*

*I'm just shell shocked, the first time I've ever had an inadvertent whistle. I go to Larry Rice, who's the ref, I said, "Larry...I blew my whistle."*

*He said, "Is there any way that you could rule that the defense recovered the ball?" I'm sitting there thinking, and I'm kind of sweating because I'm thinking, "Okay, man, you've got to do what's right. You have to do what's right." I'm pausing for a minute.*

*Here comes Bill Levy, from the other side of the field, I'll never forget this; we laugh about it all the time now. He says, "Ken, I don't know what you had but I heard a whistle all the way on the other side of the field."*

*I said, "Larry, inadvertent whistle. I'll go tell the coach on the sideline." So I walk over to this coach and he's a good guy, I really liked this guy a lot. He was on the hot seat. I went right up to him and I looked him right in the eye and said, "Coach, I blew an inadvertent whistle. I apologize for that but you're not going to be able to keep the ball; it's got to go back to the other team."*

*He looks at me very quiet, he kind of puts his mouth to my ear and says, "Ken, I like you, I understand you made a mistake and I appreciate you owning up to it. But I've got to tell you my job is on the line, and I'm just disappointed that you made that mistake."*

*Well of course, as luck would have it on that series the guy gets the ball back, goes back in for the winning touchdown and that coach is fired the next day. I'm thinking to myself, "Oh, my God. Here I am my third year in, I have an inadvertent whistle," so I'm internalizing, right? I'm internalizing that I cost the coach the job, which I didn't, but I had made that call.*

*What always stuck with me after that was the importance of being honest with everything you do in your officiating life, and always telling the truth no matter how much it hurts. Realize that coaches' jobs are on the line on every call that you make, and you've got to do the best you can to be the most prepared, to learn to be focused, to not lose concentration, which happened on that play. That affected me for the rest of my career, the rest of my 16 years on the field. It's certainly had an impact on how I approach things as a coordinator.*

# Chapter 6

**The Focus Formula:** *Evolution of a Football Official*

◆━━━━━━━━━━━━━━━━━━━━━━━━━━◆

*"Diligence is the mother of good luck."* - Benjamin Franklin

In Chapter 3, we covered the Focus Factors needed to develop into a top level football official. Then, in Chapter 4, we discussed how a person might get started in football officiating. Now we need to examine the path to take you from your current situation towards your eventual goal.

It should be noted that individual goals will differ at this juncture. While people may desire different outcomes as they pursue their goals, the process remains quite the same. I call this The Focus Formula.

Those reading this book familiar with the avocation will easily recall several officials that achieved their goals of officiating football at the highest levels but will also conjure an even longer list of those who fell short of their dreams. I want to take a moment to examine the differences between those two distinct lists.

I believe this concept has applications outside the officiating world also. Researching this book on how to become the best football official has reaffirmed those beliefs. Regardless of the level to which you aspire: Varsity, NCAA or NFL; it depends simply on one person – YOU.

You see, at the end of the day, the success of your officiating career will be entirely in your hands. There are no shortcuts, no magic potion, and no pixie dust to sprinkle around. The people who are at the top are there because they deserve to be there. Sure there are exceptions. There always will be. But those exceptions are far outweighed by the men and women that have worked hard, set lofty and challenging goals and then got straight to the arduous task of achieving them.

So I caution you at this point. Many have gone before you on somewhat similar journeys. Few have successfully reached their destination. The choice is yours. Take responsibility for your actions, your future and the road that leads from today towards your dreams. Or you can start creating excuses that will feebly support why you didn't reach those dreams. It relies simply on YOU.

The Focus Formula consists of three distinct and important pillars which form the foundation of every successful official's development plan:

- The Official as a Person
- The Official's Experience
- Networking and Promotion

**Personal Development**

Let's assume for the moment that you have completed each of the steps I've outlined to this point. If you are a more veteran official, please bear with me as you most likely are further along at this point in your officiating career. The steps were:

1. Ride-a-long with an experienced official

2. Joined your local association

3. Worked some games

4. Found a mentor

Continuous improvement, by definition, never ends. You must develop an action plan to take you from your current position to your ultimate goal. The only way to reach the NFL or Division I level is to deliberately and purposefully plan to improve your officiating game to game, season to season, year to year. There are no shortcuts and no freebies. The heights to which you soar are a direct and proportional reflection of the effort expended in achieving those heights. The NFL isn't raffling off those 120 roster spots and Rogers Redding isn't giving away SEC jobs on a first come, first served basis; they are earned by the world's best football officials.

Let me explain this in another way and I have to give NFL replay official Tommy Moore full credit for enlightening me. Take two officials that start their careers in the same year. The first, we'll call him Joe, likes football, thinks the money is okay, attends association meetings but feels they are a waste of time. Joe is pretty motivated to get to the high school varsity level and works reasonably hard the first three years to get that first varsity assignment. As he enters his fourth year, Joe feels like he's "made it" and his motivation begins to wane. Joe doesn't work on his fitness or his rules knowledge in the off-season choosing to wait until the season starts. Joe enters his fourth season about 15 pounds overweight but promises to lose it once the season starts. During the association's video review sessions, Joe likes to poke fun at the officials in the clips. Joe also becomes increasingly bitter about the quality of his schedule believing he should be getting "better" games. Joe believes he is excluded from the "cliché" and that you must be in the good old boy's network to advance.

Fred, the other official, reaches the varsity level in the same amount of time as Joe. Fred has also reached out to a veteran official who he met during his first year while officiating a youth league game. Fred liked this official's' coaching and constructive criticism from the onset asked if he would be willing to mentor a new official. Fred maintains this relationship with his mentor shadowing him in his varsity games, participating in informal rules study and watching film of the mentor's college games each week. Fred sets a goal of officiating a first round playoff game in his state in his fourth year and enrolls in an officiating clinic in the spring.

Fred dedicates himself to a 12 month fitness plan and starts a rules study group with 3 other fellow officials from January to July. They meet once per month on Sunday afternoon for a few hours. Fred's chosen position is Back Judge and he asks the association's president; who are the top 3 back judge officials. Fred invites each to lunch over the months leading up to his fifth season in order to ask detailed questions, review philosophical tenants of the position and basically "pick their brain." One of these officials takes an interest to Fred and provides Fred with a variety of film clips on pass interference to review and even offers to attend one of Fred's upcoming JV games and observe his performance. Fred volunteers to help with his association's annual dinner and at the close of season five receives a second round play-off assignment. This provides Fred an incredible amount of motivation and he seeks out a camp in a nearby state which offers NFL and NCAA instructors as well as live snaps. Fred is nominated to run for the Board of Director's in year six.

Now each of us can probably relate to Joe and Fred. We may know Joe and Fred personally. Both Joe and Fred are really good guys. Both are good officials. But here is the difference. Fred makes a conscious effort to improve each and every year. Fred sets goals and develops action plans to improve.

Joe, on the other hand, reaches a ceiling and finds it difficult to advance his career. Joe's improvement stalls, his skills fail to improve each year. Joe remains a third year official in year four, in year five and in year six. Unless Joe changes his course of action he may always be a third year official or worse…he may quit officiating all together.

The big difference between Joe and Fred is how they respond to the events that most certainly present themselves to every football official at some point in their career. I call this the Rule of 90/10. 10% of everything that happens in officiating is the event itself. 90% is how you react to the event.

Fitness, rules knowledge, mechanics, and involvement in the local association…these are components to every official's career but Fred and Joe chose remarkably different methods to deal with each.

Your personal development as an official is, by far, the single most important element of the Focus Formula. As shown in the diagram, it's the foundation on which the rest of your officiating career lies. You may notice the Focus Formula appears as a triangle. You must concentrate the majority of your effort on personal development. You can't put more effort into Networking and Promotion in effect up-ending the triangle. Without that foundation, the pyramid will crumble. Your career, regardless of the heights you pursue, rests on your personal development.

## Experience - During the Season

As you enter each season, your focus must be on continuous improvement. A typical high school official may receive 20-30 games plus another 20 games if you work youth leagues. Keep a log of each and every game you officiate noting dates, teams and fellow officials. Assess your performance following each game, noting play situations where rules interpretations or mechanics were in question. Commit to following up with your mentor or the rule book specific to these situations so you understand what happened and are better prepared for repeat situations. Break your season into quarters and set realistic goals for you self-improvement in each quarter. Evaluate your performance against those goals after each game.

For example, you might chose dead-ball officiating or proper signaling as an area to work on. Select two or three such goals and concentrate on improving your game. Ask for feedback from your crew members, observers and your mentor. As you improve a specific skill, think ahead and plan the next set of goals you can accomplish in the coming weeks. Were there emotional reactions to your calls? How were your positioning, your attitude, and your own emotions? Create a mental checklist and hold yourself accountable.

Video review may be the only way to thoroughly debrief every situation on the field. Through video, you can witness positioning, mechanics, the call, the position of your partners, the action of the play.

I have discussed the importance of video in a previous chapter so I won't beleaguer the point here. Ask one hundred high school football officials and you might find ten that actively review their game film. Ask one hundred Division I officials and you will find that one hundred review their film. You want to separate yourself from the competition? Develop a system for obtaining your game film and break it down each week. Don't make excuses for why you can't get it! Ask your best friend, spouse or mom to film you. Reach out to the school staff to get copies of your games. Just get the film, break it down and watch your improvement skyrocket game to game.

Another thing you can do during the season is film games on TV. Now some might admonish this tactic but I've found that in every game, I can learn from the crew on the field. I make use of my rewind button and on each and every penalty; I rewind and watch the play with the penalty in mind. Did I see it on the original play at full speed? We typically watch the game as a spectator so it takes some time to train your eye to watch film as an official. I notice positioning of the officials, the players, the mechanics as the play develops. I pay particular attention to body language, signaling and demeanor of the crew members. Do I agree with the call? Did I notice a technique that could improve my officiating? How did the referee communicate the penalty and enforcement? What did his signals communicate to those watching?

So much can be learned from watching those officials at the higher levels. In the simplest form, if we want to reach those levels, we need to study those that have and adopt components their game that can improve our own.

**Experience - The Off-Season**

You survived the football season. What's next? You might be tempted to take a month or two off, watch some college of pro football on TV, and wind down during the holidays. But now is truly the time to buckle down and get to work. Start looking ahead to next season NOW and you'll be miles ahead of your competition. Officiating football at the highest levels is a 12 month commitment.

The off-season can be used to your advantage if you are proactive in how you approach it. Conduct a sincere and unbiased self-assessment. Plan to attend a spring camp or clinic. Join or start a rules study group.

Identify and prioritize your off-season development. Ask these questions of yourself:

- Does my physical fitness need improvement?

- Can I improve my athletic look?

- What is my weight situation?

- How do I run? Can it be improved?

- Can I work in signaling, rules knowledge, and game management?

- What are three main areas of my game I want to improve before next season?

- What hurdles might get in the way of accomplishing those goals?

The off-season is a great time to improve your physical fitness and appearance. There are several months before the season starts and it's a perfect time to get into top physical condition. Confidence and a stronger self-assured presence are natural by-products of being in shape and ready for game day.

Identify some on-field issues you had during the past season and develop an action plan to improve them. Perhaps you had difficulty with holding calls on the line of scrimmage. Maybe your rules knowledge of the kicking game needs improvement. The off-season is perfect for improving such deficiencies.

Officiating can be the most humbling of avocations. Just when you think you've ready, there will be a situation, play or time which will test you and your judgment. Simply put, we never truly "arrive" at the top. NFL and NCAA officials devote countless hours to fine-tuning their skills and are the first to admit there is no such thing as the "perfect game."

The off-season is a great time to work on some of your developmental needs with your mentor. Without the demands of a weekly officiating schedule, you might find your mentor has more time to work with you on those areas that need improvement. Ask them for advice on how to improve your problem areas.

In the off-season, football doesn't offer the multitude of spring and summer games as in basketball and baseball. You might find a camp where you can get live snaps or maybe a 7-on-7 passing tournament, but the opportunities are few and far between. You do have the ability to review game film from the previous season however. If you've taken the steps to obtain your film and not made the typical excuses, you should have a small collection of games for off-season study. This is a great time to review game film in a rules study group as well. Collective wisdom and group discussion are powerful teaching tools and a perfect complement to film review.

Does your signaling need work? Have you ever actually seen yourself signal? You don't feel you have the same flair as Mike Carey or Steve Shaw? Get your video camera out again and film yourself demonstrating every signal in the signal chart. Yes, I mean **EVERY** signal. Stand in front of a full length mirror and practice. I've heard stories of NFL officials being considered for one of the prestigious referee positions have to make a trip to the great Jerry Markbreit's house. (Mr. Markbreit is currently the only person to have officiated in 4 Super Bowls and is a legend in NFL officiating.) I'm told that lengthy discussions about signaling, penalty explanations, pronunciation, even the way your hair is cut; take place in Mr. Markbreit's living room. Focusing on that level of detail isn't reserved for NFL referees. Anyone can improve on the finer points.

Don't wait until the season starts to practice your signaling. Make crisp, sharp signals a natural part of your officiating game. Improving the finer details of your game could be the key to advancement to the next level.

The time is now to begin improving all aspects of your game. You need a little help? Why not enroll in a spring training camp or clinic?

## Experience - Camps and Clinics

"On-field clinics and camp gives officials to hone their mechanics and skills and to learn form clinicians. The exposure and the opportunity to show case your skills to people who can hire you or make recommendations are unparalleled. Camps and clinics will present you with a chance to learn something new or different and you will have the chance to walk away a better official." – Vic Winnek, Great West Umpire.

Camps and clinics are a critical component of the overall development of your advancement and officiating career. There are many camps from which to choose over the United States. These training opportunities allow you to received instruction from some of the world's greatest football officials. They also allow you to network and build relationships with those same officials. Some are expensive, some take several days to complete. Some are better, some are worse. So how do you find the right camp?

First you need to do some research in order to make a good decision about what camp fits your goals and developmental needs. Determine how much time and money you have available to devote to the camp environment. What are your immediate officiating goals?

There are basically two kinds of camps: teaching camps and exposure camps. Both are valuable and have their place, but you need to understand the difference so your experience is both rewarding and beneficial. Teaching takes place at both but the level of instruction differs.

The off-season is devoted to development of your officiating skills. Early on in your career, your first consideration will be instruction in fundamentals. Finding a camp that teaches the essentials is paramount. In exposure or "try-out" camps, there are opportunities to meet conference supervisors and other key decision-makers but less focus on the basics. The expectation is that you have a solid foundation of the essentials and are ready to take your skills to the next level. There will certainly be teaching but it tends to be more focused on the details of this craft.

There are often multiple talent scouts at the exposure camps and they serve as a great vehicle to showcase your officiating skills in your attempts to climb the ladder. They are definitely a valuable component of every aspiring official's career but your number one priority is to address the developmental needs you had at the end of the previous season. Get your game ready for that next level and there will be a proper time and place for the exposure camp in your future.

I won't attempt to recommend one camp over another. Rather, I'll give you a checklist on how to choose a camp. If you will follow this simple method, you can use it to choose a camp or clinic for years to come.

In addition to the two previously discussed camp types, I want to point out two additional classifications: Classroom and Field Instruction. Due to the limited availability of spring football, some camps are conducted in a classroom-only mode. Others guarantee live snaps on the field at colleges and universities when teams are conducting spring scrimmages. Both can be valuable learning experiences and I wanted to point out this difference as we discuss our checklist.

## ➤ Who are the Instructors?

The quality of the camp is directly proportional to the staff. You want to be taught by successful officials and from officials that have achieved those levels to which you aspire.

## ➤ Instructor to Student Ratio

Just like in a normal class room, this ratio can have an impact on your ability to receive feedback and individualized attention. Ask about the number of clinicians and the expected number of trainees. Live play camps will typically limit the number of students in order to maximize the number of snaps and tailor the personal instruction to the student.

There is no right number, but realize your experience in a class of 50 students with one Big Ten umpire talking about chop blocks will be much different than having an NFL line judge standing behind you on the line of scrimmage discussing pre-snap duties.

## ➢ NFHS or NCAA Mechanics

There are camps that focus strictly on each and with that comes a different level of instruction regarding each level's rules and mechanics. Understand where you are in your officiating career and what your immediate goals are so that you chose the camp format that is appropriate for your needs.

There are fewer opportunities for live play at the NFHS level due to the restrictions placed on high school student-athletes. NCAA camps often coincide with spring training and offer the ability to officiate college level play. Fundamentals are taught at both levels and it should be easy for you to choose a camp that fits your needs.

## ➢ Is there Video Review?

There are many good camps with veteran instructors. But you may never see yourself on video. Ask about the availability of video review. Coordinating video during a camp experience is a monumental task and many camps do not offer this tool. But I believe it's a necessary part of the optimal camp experience. Not only from your development watching your own video, but working with those NCAA and NFL officials on *how* to break down your film will accelerate your advancement and learning for years to come.

## ➢ Is there Classroom Instruction?

Some camp formats only offer classroom instruction and this type of camp is perfect for the less experienced official. Often the Field Training camps complement the training with the classroom to review play situations, film and other teaching points. Classroom only camps typically are one day in length and start off with a key-note speaker followed by breakout sessions by position and/or emphasis on a skill such as goal line plays.

## ➤ Will You Receive Written Evaluations of Field Work?

Written critiques should be very helpful to identify some of your strong and weak points. Most often, camp instructors will see some small intangible need for you to improve upon that you may not have known. They will also provide excellent insight and advice on what to expect at the higher levels giving you a clear path on what you need to address as you seek advancement.

## ➤ Are there Returning Students?

Is there a waiting list? Does the website have testimonials from former students? Are there success stories where past students have been successfully advanced into higher levels? This is a true test of a camp's quality and should not go unnoticed during your evaluation. Ask those questions of the camp leadership personnel.

## ➤ Cost

Camps can range from $25 for a single day of classroom instruction to well over $1000 for 3 day clinic with live play and film review. Each can prove beneficial to every official and learning can occur in many ways.

Finding the right camp can reap rewards in your officiating career. Money and time can be wasted if your officiating goals and needs are not properly aligned with the mission of the camp itself. My intention here is to educate you to make an informed decision. The off-season camp should become an integral component in your development as an official and accelerate your progression and improvement as you pursue your officiating goals and dreams.

Camps can be a valuable resource for your improving your officiating skill set as well as providing opportunities for you to network with key decision-makers and gain much-needed exposure. As you progress in your officiating career, not only will your goals and needs change; so will your expectations of each camp environment. If you reach a point where you feel the camps you are attending are not providing value or honing your skills, you may need to seek other camps that can satisfy your expectations.

Finally, the camp environment is a great chance to associate with like-minded individuals. You will find that your mild obsession with football officiating may not be fully understood with your friends and family. Most won't truly appreciate your desire to officiate football at the highest levels. People will continually question your desires and dreams. Some may even attempt to discourage you from pursuing those dreams. Camps provide you a unique opportunity to surround yourself with similar motivated people passionate about officiating football. This environment is conducive to learning and improvement. The people you will meet and associations you make will reach beyond the short camp schedule and provide you meaningful relationships in and out of the officiating community.

## Developing Your Game and Schedule

A signification component of your experience in the Focus Formula is the development of a quality and meaningful schedule. You should view your schedule season to season as an extension of your personal development. Understand that many components with regards to the games you officiate will be beyond your control. Others are within your circle of influence and rely squarely upon your shoulders. You can control your athletic look, your run, your mannerisms, your decisions and your focus on continuous improvement. You can't control where your supervisor assigns your games or which crew you work on. You can't direct which teams you officiate or which stadiums you visit. Control what's within your power and release what is not.

In all honesty, your schedule may frustrate and discourage you. There will be times when you feel you deserved a better game or you think you earned a higher evaluation. Remember the evaluation and game assignment process can be subjective. Take all the assessment and guidance to heart. Your job here is very simple: Devote yourself to hard work, patience and consistency. Your dedication will most certainly pay off in the long run. The road you are traveling is littered with those that lost their focus and strayed off the path.

Let us talk about schedule quality for a moment. Quality does not mean Division I college officiating (although it would most certainly apply). Quality means working more and more competitive match-ups, games with better athletes, faster play, higher emotion. It means taking every opportunity to work football games that both fit your current level as well as those that are at a level to which you aspire. Your schedule should be a reflection of your journey and show continuous improvement with regards to your game assignments as well.

In my local area, Catholic school youth football is very popular. The football is very competitive and has a long and distinguished history in our community. Each year, the local Catholic school league championships are played at one of the prominent high schools towards the end of the season. As a rookie official, we were assigned to work the chains in these games my first year. I distinctly remember the roar of the crowd, the electricity in the air, the passion on the faces of coaches, players and officials alike. I decided that day that I wanted to work a youth league championship game in my near future. I set a goal that was a stretch, but was definitely in my reach.

Notice I didn't decide that day that I wanted to officiate a state play-off championship or make it as an SEC official. Sure I have had thoughts about those things. Those are both admirable goals; however I wanted a target I could work towards and hopefully obtain in a reasonable amount of time. I encourage you to set your sights in a similar fashion. Push yourself but also set yourself up for success rather than failure. I see too many officials get discouraged and quit because they don't reach their goals fast enough.

I began formulating a make-shift game plan on the sidelines that day. I pondered what I needed to do to prepare for next year and what steps I would need to take to put myself in the best possible position as a second year official. I vividly recall watching a gentleman work the line judge position (which most rookie officials work their first year) and was very impressed with his officiating. I can still see that official on the sidelines working his game and being very impressed with what I saw. He had IT and IT was obvious. I made a point to approach him after the game and tell him he made an impression upon me. Just watching great officials at work, enjoying the moment and experiencing the thrill of that championship game cemented in my mind that I wanted to be in that same place one day.

So you work on your schedule quality each game, each season. Work as many games as possible. Never turn back a game unless it is absolutely necessary. Work hard to improve your skills and your schedule will naturally improve as a result of your efforts and it will not go unnoticed. Make yourself available and be flexible. You never know when you may get that call.

## Networking & Promotion

Networking is the third Focus Formula ingredient. Promotion sounds self-centered and vain but it's really about networking and accentuating your positives.

Networking is defined as meeting or communicating with new people or within a group. Networking is not schmoozing. Networking is building strong relationships with people in the football officiating community. Ultimately you want your fellow officials to respect you and your game. You want to be a good team player, get along well with others and always give back. Be yourself and realize you can't control everything. These efforts will be repaid with positive referrals and recommendations when the time comes to advance.

If networking is the outward focus, then self-promotion is looking inside. Understand that as you move up the ladder of officiating success, the stakes get higher and the pressure mounts. You should consider this advancement path similar to a job search. There will always be positions open in various conferences at all levels. If you recall my Barrel of Monkeys theory, there are always hands pulling you up from above and your hand reaching down pulling someone else up from below. When the opportunity arises, you must be prepared.

So what is the first aspect of most every job search? A resume. I interviewed conference supervisors across the US and the majority felt a resume was a good idea. There were a few that didn't think it was necessary. However, I believe you should start building your resume immediately regardless of your current level.

Just like your professional resume, your officiating resume can easily communicate valuable information and help you gain respect from the key decision makers. It allows a chronological history of your experience, past schedules, training and accomplishments. I suggest including personal information as well. Are you married, do you have children, what is your profession and education level? Do you have interests outside of football? Of course, your football credentials are important but the decision makers want to get to know the person as well as the official. They place a tremendous amount of trust in the officials that take the field, so any information which helps them understand you as a person is helpful.

Include your athletic background and experience. Did you play in high school? Did you play any college sports? Did you receive any awards? Focus on conveying information as a well-rounded person with goals and dreams in both your professional, personal and officiating areas of your life. Many of the people I interviewed were successful in their careers and in with their families as well as on the field. As I said earlier, *success leaves traces.*

Begin building this resume early in your career. Not only will it help you recall the details easier as you build it from season to season, your resume becomes a living, breathing document which you can use as you evaluate your action plan for accomplishing your goals.

I don't suggest you send this resume out blindly to supervisors or conferences. I do suggest you include the resume with your conference application once you determine where you would like to apply. Keeping it up to date will allow you to respond in a moment's notice should the need arise.

I also believe the act of keeping your officiating resume current is a constant reminder of your goal to officiate at the highest level. When you see your career on paper, it gives you a different perspective and might possible allow you to examine your experience from a decision-maker's point of view. That could prove extremely valuable as you move forward in your officiating career.

## Applying to Conferences

You won't find a Help Wanted ad in your local newspaper on or Craig's List for college football officials. I doubt Monster or CareerBuilder sites would be of much help either. But just like a normal job, you do have to apply for a roster spot if you want to make it as an NCAA football official.

I interviewed several Division I conference supervisors during the research phase of this book and I always inquired about their particular application process. The SEC, ACC, Conference USA, Sunbelt, Ohio Valley, SWAC and Mountain West are just a few of the conferences I called. The path to officiate NCAA football is consistent and follows a remarkably simple progression. Every conference, from the NAIA through the Division I, has an application process. Some are more formal than others. A few just require an email or letter to the supervisor stating your interest in officiating in their conference. Others provide the applicant with a form to complete. Still others ask for a resume and/or video footage of your work to accompany the completed application. All conferences require the applicant to take the initiative. That means you must take action and get the wheels turning.

As you might imagine, conference supervisors receive hundreds of applications each season. I recall Doug Rhoads, ACC Coordinator, say that he had several hundred applications for 1 open roster spot in 2008. Competitive to say the least!

## But where should I apply?

I wish there was a simple answer to this question. Your geographical location will play an important role here. Do a bit of research to determine what NAIA or Division III conferences are within a 2 hour drive of your home city or town. Talk to your mentor about where most college officials prior start their careers at the next level. Interview one or two NFL or NCAA top level officials that belong to your association. Ask what path they took in their career. Ask your high school assigner. Don't leave any stones unturned.

In my particular case, I had three choices: Mid-South (NAIA), Heartland (DIII) or the WVIAC (DII). I contacted each supervisor in the winter asking about the application process and spring scrimmages. I attended the clinics for all three working scrimmages in both the Mid-South and WVIAC. All three had historically been starting points for officials in my geographic location. I was hired as a supplemental WVIAC official in April and later offered a deep wing position during the conference clinic in late July. Due to some crew changes prior to the season opener, the supervisor, Billy Alton, assigned me four games that first season which, quite honestly, was three more than I'd hoped for!

Even as a WVIAC supplemental official, I still pursued the Mid-South and Heartland conferences. I worked two games with a Northern Kentucky Mid-South crew as well as a Heartland JV game in Cincinnati. I was following the tried and true advice of my mentors: Get all the snaps you can.

Once you have a pretty good idea regarding which conferences are near your geographical location, you need to determine how prospective officials make a formal application. The internet can be a valuable tool for research. All conferences will have a website and most likely a few pages targeted on the sport of football. Many of the smaller conferences, however, will not have officiating information on these sites. They simply do not have the resources to offer officiating information via the conference website. You should be able to, at the least, find the Commissioner's office contact information and with a short phone call, have the Supervisor of Football Officials name, phone and email address at your fingertips.

Another great way to break into these smaller conferences is to attend any training clinics they may offer. For example, the Heartland Conference, Indianapolis, IN; holds a one day clinic in the May each year. The cost is nominal and the focus is entirely NCAA rules and mechanics. Larry Snyder, the supervisor of football officials, hosts the clinic each year. All attendees have the opportunity to meet Larry as well as join his mailing list where he published rules quizzes, bulletins, and mechanics updates throughout the year. Larry holds a short session specifically geared to those wishing to become college football officials. He discusses his application process and allows for questions. This is a fantastic method to get on Larry's radar screen and prepare to possibly officiate football in the Heartland Conference.

You will find similar circumstances as you gain entry to the NAIA and DIII conferences around the country. Some will not have a clinic, some will not have a formal application process…all are seeking qualified applicants for their conferences. All lose officials to promotion and retirement each year and therefore need to keep a steady stream of prospects coming in the front door. I call this the NCAA "Harvest" and it happens every April to May following the spring scrimmages. Seeds have been planted and the time comes to reap what you've sown. That is how I got my first break and it's a great way for you to kick-start your college officiating career.

A bit of advice here – Don't wait for it to happen. Don't be fooled by thinking that once you are ready someone will walk up to you at a game and say "Wow, would you like to officiate college football?" It is imperative that you set goals, develop a strategy and take action. G.S.A: Goals, Strategy, Action. At the end of the day, your officiating career and advancement rests in your hands.

# *Zebra Tales*

Kavin McGrath, Big East Head Linesman

*I'll never forget December 1, 2001; shortly after 9/11. I got assigned to the Army/Navy game in Philadelphia and President Bush is going to be there so we got Secret Service everywhere. We get in the locker room and they say President Bush is going to flip the coin. The Secret Service agents came in and said "We know exactly where you're supposed to be standing so just don't move around. There's going to be so many people out there when the president comes out we want you to stand still."*

*My position is on the sideline, the Navy sideline at the 50 yard line and here comes President Bush from the other sideline. He comes out and there's his entourage and he goes out and does his thing and I thought that was pretty cool. I saw a President!*

*The President always sits one side first half and the other side the second half. He's going to sit on Navy sideline the first half so when he gets done with the coin toss he's walking down the 50 yard line right at me. I thought ok here we go. He's got his Secret Service agents and he walks right up to me and shakes my hand. I tap him on the back and he taps me on the back and I said "Thanks for coming, Mr. President." I don't even remember what I said but that was probably the biggest thing in my life whether you like President Bush or not it's still the President of the United States.*

*Lo and behold somebody has a picture of it. I've got it hung in my basement with me and President Bush shaking hands at the 50 yard line Army Navy game. It was shortly after 9/11 so the emotions were pretty high.*

*Then, President Bush went on up in the stands and there's this lady Secret Service agent standing right next to me still and I was feeling pretty good. I'm walking 3 feet off the ground. I just got to shake the President's hand and I turn around to her and make a little comment like "Well what would you have done if I body slammed him?" She didn't take too kindly to that! She gave me an evil look. She didn't answer me. I said "I don't think I should've said that."*

*That was probably the biggest thing in my career - being able to shake the President of the United States hand on the 50 yard line at the Army Navy game shortly after 9/11. Somebody at the Navy archives had a picture of us. Somebody found it for me and I've got it hanging in my basement.*

# Chapter 7
## The Journey to DI and Beyond

*"When you don't know where you are going, all roads lead there."* —Todd
Skaggs

I'm going to step out on a limb here. I believe we have this topic of advancement entirely backwards.

As an aspiring high school official I became interested in taking this avocation to a higher level in my fifth year. Truth be known I was interested in the higher levels of officiating in my rookie year but my class of new officials was discouraged from asking questions about college or NFL officiating. As I got to know more of my fellow officials I became acquainted with those that officiated at higher levels. My local association is fortunate to have many NCAA and NFL officials past and present. Yet still less experienced officials are told to focus on the current level. I truly believe this is a mistake and actually has an adverse effect on football officials in their formative years.

As each season passed, I heard about other officials that were earning roster spots on NAIA and NCAA Division III college crews but I was never really sure how those decisions were made. In fact, I wasn't even sure who to ask or where to go for information. Now mind you I knew I wasn't ready to move up. Far from it indeed but I was definitely interested!

Why not encourage every rookie official to set goals of officiating in the Big East, PAC-10 or NFL? Set the expectation that you must excel at the lower levels in order to rise to the top. Imagine if our coaching counterparts told the freshman squad to forget about varsity football. Don't even ask questions about college, it will take care of itself. To become a successful college or professional player, the preparation and training begins years prior to signing the intent letter or rookie contract.

I like to plan and educate myself in order to prepare for such an activity and I found that there weren't many resources out there that offered help or information. You certainly couldn't Google "how to become a college football official" and get very far!

Attrition is very high amongst football officials in their early years. Some don't understand the commitment level required to be successful. Others can't afford the time required. Only a select few actually make it through the first few years and officiate a varsity contest.

Yet rookies are enamored by the thought of officiating in the SEC or NFL. Some recruits enter with those goals in mind and we tell them to put those dreams on hold. Why not take the opposite approach? Parade your association's successful officials into the rookie class on opening night. Let them share their career paths, their post season bowl games they've worked, the thrill of walking into a stadium of 80,000 raving fans. Then help the rookies realize these people are just normal, ordinary people who each got their start in similar meeting years ago. Teach the new officials that all successful officiating careers begin on a pee wee field in Anytown, USA. All NFL officials worked JV and varsity high school ball games. Every BCS National Championship official had probably worked a middle school championship at some point in their career. Stress that everyone starts the same way and that each person in that room has an equal opportunity to rise to the same level.

What I've learned in the past year and a half of studying officials and discussing their careers applies to everyone reading this book. Any of you can make it to the top of this avocation. It takes hard work, dedication, self-confidence and time. Rising to the top is not easy and it's not fast but at every level, when you step out on that field for the first time as you've achieved those milestone goals, you become a rookie all over. There are varsity rookies, DIII rookies, DI rookies and NFL rookies. And guess what? You get goose bumps on opening kick-off at all rookie levels of football officiating!

## *Zebra Tales*

Gerald Austin, Conference USA Coordinator of Football
Officiating and former NFL Referee

*Probably one of the better stories is when Bill Parcells was at the Jets, and on a kickoff return his receiver catches the ball and runs it back to midfield. But I've got a flag for holding and I've got to take this. So I turn on the microphone and I said "During the return, holding on the receiving team, 10 yards. It'll be a first down."*

*Bill's hollering "What's the number? If you can make the call you've got to have the number." Well it just so happens we go to a TV timeout. We're backed up on timeouts so we go to a TV timeout.*

*I go over there and he says "Jerry, now you made the call. You gotta have a number." I said "Bill, I didn't see the number but I saw the foul, and it was 30-something."*

*Bill looked at me with as straight a face as you've ever seen and he says "30-something? That's a TV show. What I want is the number of the player that committed the foul." Then he starts laughing and I start laughing.*

# Chapter 8

## Advanced Focus Factors: *Next Level*

*"Begin with the end in mind."* -- Steven Covey

O ver the course of my research, I detected similar qualities that were present in both the top football officials as well as the characteristics sought by supervisors. Improving on these intangibles will help you refine your approach to officiating football at the highest levels. In some respect you might feel this is splitting hairs, but I suggest to you that what might separate the top ten percent from the bottom ninety percent is a relentless focus on improving the small aspects.

Great football officials don't just happen by accident. Use this checklist to conduct a self-evaluation. Imagine a Division I supervisor sitting in the stands evaluating several prospects. Each of these advanced Focus Factors may well be criteria for evaluation. Consider this list a report card, or as at work – a performance appraisal. Be honest as you evaluate your performance then set goals for improvements in areas you feel need additional work.

It is this same persistent pursuit of perfection needed to excel in officiating, and in life.

### On-The-Field Factors

The first six factors can be observed sitting in the stands. They comprise less than half of the advanced Focus Factors, however your progress will be limited if you don't have all six.

1.  **Credibility** - Do coaches and players believe your decisions? Do the coaches and players trust your decision making ability?

Credibility takes years and years to cultivate and seconds to lose. Officials new to each level of advancement have their credibility rating reset to zero. The key to gaining credibility is being consistent. You will begin to develop trust with the coaches and players over time. Credibility doesn't hurt with your supervisor either.

2.  **Officiating Knowledge** – Are you fundamentally sound in all aspects of officiating (rules, mechanics, fitness, etc.)?

Mastering the craft of football officiating requires you to understand the rules and how to properly apply those rules in a variety of situations. Don Lucas, Sunbelt, believes you must become a student of the rules. It's a given. You will hear veterans discuss the *intent of the rule*. You must decide early in your career to be a "rules man" and dedicate yourself to this each and every season. The gym and track must become a part of your daily routine. Successful officials nail down the mechanics of their position to ensure they are in the correct place to make the call. All requires a constant attention to learning and improving your officiating skill set.

3.  **Game Management Skills** – Are you aware of the game clock, down and distance, game flow, and potential game decisions?

    Great game management does not happen once you hit the DI or NFL levels. It starts right now. Game management goes beyond spotting fouls or penalties, positioning or teamwork with your crew. You must hone your awareness of the clock, emotions, and tone of the game. You must be able to anticipate the future and be prepared for what is just ahead of the next snap.

4.  **Conflict Resolution** – Can you respond appropriately in a professional manner?

    You MUST be able to effectively handle conflict as you advance. Your advancement will be halted if you can't communicate with coaches and players. All positions on the crew interact with coaches and players constantly throughout the game and how you handle these interactions can play a huge role in your overall performance.

5. **Leadership** – What can your crew mates and supervisor expect from you? Are you a professional? Do you bring the same level of preparation to each game?

Ask yourself this question. Do other officials that work with you want to be as good as you are? Are you a source for information? Study those officials around you today. Who are the leaders? Who do you look up to and seek out for information? Be that person.

6. **Be a Good Crew Member** – How do you prioritize the game, crew and yourself?

It's often been said that when you step out on the field, your only friends are those wearing the stripes. I can't emphasize enough the importance of being a team player. I could devote a chapter to team officiating; I've heard it stressed so much from those top officials interviewed. Nothing is more important than protecting the integrity of the game. We are the custodians, the caretakers. Next is the crew. We rely on each other every play. Our mechanics are designed to complement each position and area of responsibility. We have no safety nets once the play is blown ready.

**Off-The-Field Factors**

Each Conference Supervisor stressed the need to evaluate prospects away from the game. They wanted to know more than just the official. They wanted to know the person. I know very few successful officials that are not excellent in these areas.

7.  **Off-Season Preparation** - Do you take the steps necessary in the off-season to arrive prepared for week one? Are you professional in your approach to each consecutive season?

There are many variables in advancing to the higher levels of football officiating. Some you control, some you do not. You should have noticed by now that being on the top of this craft is a 12 month obligation. How you approach your off-season speaks volumes with regard to how you will perform when game time arrives.

8.  **Be A Team Player** – Do you work towards improving your crew?

Yes, this is both an on and off-field factor. Your participation in meetings, pre-game, training, camps & clinics are all factors to be considered. There are no islands in football officiating. Supervisors want officials that are positive additions to their staff. Crews want members that add value and gel with the other members.

9.  **Physical Conditioning** – Do you maintain an athletic look and proper conditioning?

By and large, officials at the DI and NFL levels have an athletic presence. Physical fitness will continue to have a huge impact on hiring as well as keeping your spot on staff. Getting in shape and staying there take work and dedication. This commitment has a natural tendency to cross over into your officiating game as well.

10. **Game Preparation** – The higher you advance, the more detailed the game preparation becomes. How do you approach each game?

As an NFL and NCAA officials, it becomes a seven day cycle. Regardless of level, officials have detailed preparation plans that differ depending on which conference you work. All have concrete guidelines that begin with a postgame analysis and end the following week with a comprehensive pre-game meeting. There are multiple steps in between. You must follow a consistent course of action week-in and week-out to prepare to work football at the highest levels.

11. **Crew Mentality** – How do you interact with your crew mates off the field?

You will find nothing will negatively impact your advancement faster that a reputation for being a poor crew member. How you interact with fellow officials off the field is immediately noticed. If you are the new guy (and we all will be at some point), participate unselfishly. Do whatever it takes to be a great member of your crew. Everyone is watching.

**12. Leadership** – Can you motivate others? Can you influence and win support? Can you improve others around you?

Yes, leadership is another on- and off-field factor. Can you see the trend here? Supervisors are constantly seeking leaders. Every aspect of your officiating career is evaluated with respect to your ability to lead others and it doesn't require a white hat either.

**13. Dependability** – Can we count on you?

If you can't be trusted with small deadlines, you probably can't be trusted to make the call when the game is on the line. How can you expect a bowl game assignment or state playoff championship if you can't send in your membership dues on time? This is really simple stuff here. Do have a tendency to turn back games? Do you arrive at the game early? Do you meet the weekly crew task assignments consistently? Trust and respect are gained over time and with small consistent steps. Begin earning that trust on day one.

# *Zebra Tales*

Jim Augustyn, Arena Football League Regional Supervisor and former Big Ten official

*We had the Southern California vs. Ohio State game at Ohio State. It was in like late September. At halftime the athletic director came out and told us that there was a possibility that big storms were coming and that he thought we could get the game in. Well, I mean it wasn't ten minutes into the third quarter and it started to pour, and there was a little bit of lightning. I was a relatively new umpire in the Big Ten at that time and my crew chief was a veteran official but new to the referee position. So we had lightning, and we called timeout and said we were going to put the teams in the locker room. Unbeknownst to us, one of the veteran referees had suspended a game at Purdue that afternoon and we had the national TV game, you know a 3:30 kickoff. So he called the coaches together and they said "No, let's just play right on through it."*

*So we did, we played through it. So late in the ballgame, there was probably a minute and a half to go and Ohio State scored and it was just this huge flash of lightning. So the referee called the two coaches back and said "This is it, we're suspending the game now. We'll bring you back when the lighting clears." The Ohio State coach, he said "No, I'll tell you what. We're going to try an onside kick." Southern Cal's coach said "With a minute and a half to go? Christ." OSU's coach said "If we get the ball then suspend the game, but if they get it heck, the game's over." So he said "Okay." The Southern Cal coach was right there, and everybody knew he was going to have an onside kick. So they tried the onside kick, Southern Cal fell on it and the referee makes the announcement.  He says "By mutual agreement of both coaches the game is over."*

*We ran for this tunnel where there was a squad car waiting for us and a van, and we took off. We went back to the Woody Hayes Building and we were taking a shower. Keith Jackson's on TV saying "Well, we're still awaiting word.  We're not sure if this game is postponed or is it cancelled or what?" Here we are taking showers! So we knew it was cancelled.*

*Later we watched the coach's show at 11:00 at night back at the hotel. We're sitting there watching the show.  They asked the coach "Well, this is 100 years of Ohio State football, and they've lost games but they've always played a full 60 minutes.  Why did we only play 58 minutes and 36 seconds?"  The coach responded, "Well, the officials didn't explain it to me very clearly," when in fact he was the one that told us "No, if they fall on the ball the game's over. So let's get out of here!"*

# Chapter 9
## Two Minute Drill

O ver the past year I've intensely studied over 50 top level football officials and conference supervisors. Some of those have gone on to officiate in Super Bowls, BCS National Championship games or high school state playoff championships. Others have chosen to pursue a supervisory role overseeing the officiating for various college conferences. Each person was unique yet I continued to notice subtle similarities. As I examined my own short career I could see different aspects, both pros and cons, of my life that have an impact on my officiating and how my officiating has had an impact on my life.

This book has focused heavily on what it takes to be a successful football official at the college level. But as I reflect back on my seven year career, I realized if I had to hang up my whistle tomorrow I would be pleased with my accomplishments. John McGrath, Super Bowl veteran, said if he had to leave the NFL tomorrow, he'd be on a youth league field the next weekend working a game. So true. While I still have dreams of taking my game to the next level, of pushing the envelope just a bit more; I appreciate where each of you are in your journey. I fully understand that our goals will be different and accomplishment comes in many shapes and forms. This list of attributes transcends football officiating at every level regardless of your aspirations. It is about how I express my life through my officiating. It is about me as a person, a husband, a dad and I hope…an all-around good guy.

## #1: Live in the Now

Football is a fantastic game and we love the sport. Officiating at any level is a tremendous experience. The camaraderie amongst your fellow officials and sharing the field with them will undoubtedly provide some of the most special memories. You will remember some of those games forever.

Just before kick-off at each game, I ask you to take pause. Spend a short 10 seconds soaking up the moment. When you meet your crew out in the middle of the field, savor your time and enjoy where you are. Appreciate the hard work and effort it took to arrive at this place and taste it.

## #2: Control What You Can. Let Go of the Rest.

I suspect this principle has allowed me to get closer to my goals than any other. What can I control? I can't control my assigner's feelings, I can't control a coach's emotions, I can't control roster openings or promotions within my conference.

I can control my physical fitness, my weight, my rules knowledge, my attitude towards critique and feedback, my willingness to learn, my work ethic.

Let go of what you can't control and focus that energy towards aspects of officiating and your life that are within your influence and control. Your progress and peace of mind could certainly depend on it.

## #3: Don't be "That Guy"

We all know great partners, admirable citizens, or as my grandmother said "good people." I'm sure you've run into the opposite over the years too.

Be a good sport and a team player. Be reliable and trustworthy. An official your crew can count on. Be proud to don the stripes and share the field.

Life is too short for complainers, negative influences, drama and distraction. Don't be "that guy."

## #4: Be a Chameleon

One thing is certain about football. The game has, and will continue to, change. We must change with it. Don't let it pass you by. Be open to change and resist the urge to balk or languish. Find solace in the moment and look forward to the horizon with excitement.

Forcing ourselves into uncharted territory can only lead to growth and development. Learn to roll with the punches. People, rules interpretations, the level of play…all this will change each and every year. Embrace this and allow your willingness to develop a level of flexibility work to you advantage. Work all crew positions, readily accept new challenges, push yourself and you will be prepared when the unexpected call arrives.

## #5: As Axl Rose Sang, "Just a Little Patience."

We never advance fast enough; achieve our goals at a speed we desire, reach heights within our timetable. It is in our nature to want everything right now yet not be willing to devote the necessary time to realize our desires. Success in football officiating is paid for in advance.

Go confidently in the direction of your dreams and keep your goals in front of you. Don't let a lack of patience frustrate you or detract you from your mission. It's a marathon, not a sprint. When having difficulty, refer to #1 above.

## #6: Referee Big

As a matter of course, officials don't want to be noticed. Yet there are defining moments in every official's career and they tend to involve bang-bang plays. You must be willing to make the call. You have to crave it. The way the play slows down for you so you can see every aspect develop from start to finish. You have to want to make the big call and get it right.

Moving up in the ranks can be daunting and challenging task. You will ultimately find your officiating comfort zone.

Will you push past it and seek the challenges that present themselves as you push the envelope? You will be criticized, scolded and rejected. Will you find the resolve to step up and do what's necessary? People will be watching. Referee BIG.

# *Zebra Tales*

Gary McCarthy, Northeast-10 Field Judge

*I'll give you a story from my first year of college officiating. We had a game up in Maine, and in my first year I wasn't assigned to a crew so I floated week to week; one week I was a side judge, next week I was a back judge, etc. And we're up in Maine and we had a game up there and I was a back judge assigned to the game. As luck would have it the play clocks didn't work so they had to keep the play clock on the field. Okay, this was a seven man crew. Now in prior years the field judge in a six man crew, I believe, is the one who kept the play clock, and I'll get back to why I stated that.*

*The home team is on the five yard line and they are looking to score. I have my hand up in the air and I'm counting down, you know, three, two, one…Then I throw my flag for a delay of game. We back them up five and on the next play they score. So, after the point I head over to the home team sideline, which is our mechanic, to jog up to my free kick position. As I'm heading over to the sideline the head coach for the team that just scored is screaming at the top of his lungs "Where's my back judge!? Where's my back judge?!" So I said, "Oh, boy."*

*So I go over to him and say, "I'm here coach, what can I do for you?" He says, "Delay of game? My quarterback said he didn't see your hand up!" I said "Coach, my hand was up." I said, "It was up. I didn't see your quarterback looking at me." I'm assuming that in prior years, when they were used to a six man crew the quarterback was probably looking at the field judge. So he's going, "Your hand wasn't up!"*

I said, "It certainly was Coach and I didn't see him looking at me." After a brief delay he said, "A guy as good looking as you? He wasn't looking at you?" Then he cracks a smile and I just knew he was just busting my chops. So he smiled. I smiled and I jogged to my pre-kick position. That was an interesting play that happened. That was the first time that I realized that coaches like to have fun too.

# Chapter 10

## 4<sup>th</sup> **Quarter:** *Because 99 Won't*

Zig Ziglar said fulfillment in life is obtained when you focus your efforts on helping others achieve their goals, ambitions and dreams. That's the core of this book. Helping others like me. Football officiating has brought me a treasure chest of fond memories and lasting friendships but more importantly officiating has helped me grow personally and professionally.

I am often asked why I like to officiate sports. I find it difficult to express in words. Over the seasons, games and snaps; football officiating has become a part of my DNA. I enjoy being the custodian of the rulebook. I relish being calm, cool and collected when the world seems to be crumbling around me. I love putting on the stripes and taking the field. Very few people will ever experience the game of football from our vantage point. I truly believe it is reserved for a special breed of person and we football officials share an innate desire to immerse ourselves in the game of football. Most will simply not understand what it means to be a football official.

I often say if you hit .300 over your baseball career it will land you in Cooperstown. Try getting into the Big 12 or SEC by calling 3 out of 10 plays correctly! Our fraternity dressed in zebra stripes is comprised of dedicated, focused, passionate individuals who come together for a few hours each week and attempt to work the perfect game. We collectively strive for perfection but instead settle for excellence. It's what we do.

I want to leave you with a story about a mindset that I developed and applied to the last two years of my officiating career. It has served me well and I strongly believe is a primary factor in my relative success.

Entering the season as a WVIAC supplemental official, I maintained my back judge position on my local high school crew. I was excited about working Fuzzy Klusman's crew knowing he would challenge me and improve my officiating over the course of the season. My college goal was to work just one NCAA game my rookie year. I didn't have lofty expectations. Just one game.

I must point out here that I live in Kentucky and the WVIAC games are primarily in West Virginia. I knew I would have to work Friday night high school games and subsequently drive to the WVIAC game site arriving no later than 10 am for a Saturday contest. No worries – my mentor John Oslica had paved the way for me years before. If he could do it then so could I. Schedules were published following the WVIAC clinic and I was fortunate to receive 4 games. You can imagine my enthusiasm and excitement when I saw the schedule.

I recall the first night when I had to leave around 10:30 pm to drive to Wheeling, WV about six hours from Louisville, KY. My high school crew mates thought I was crazy. Why in the world would you want to drive until 4 am to get to a football game? No one in their right mind would do such a thing. The first two hours of that initial road trip were easy. Adrenalin kept me wide-eyed as I anticipated what my first NCAA game would bring. During that ride, I kept thinking about my friends and fellow officials comments. It was on some highway in Ohio past midnight that it hit me.

## 1 Will, 99 Won't.

I realized that if you took 100 officials and asked if they would drive six hours through the night to get to the next game – 1 will, 99 won't. Most just don't have the passion or dedication needed to truly excel in officiating. I began to see patterns in the careers of those successful officials in my research that supported this statistic.

## 1 Will, 99 Won't.

The percentages play out in most all aspects of officiating. Take the 12 month rules study: 1 will, 99 won't. What about dedication to staying physical fit? 1 will. 99 won't. Commitment to continual learning through camps and clinics? 1 will. 99 won't. Never saying no to working a game? 1 will. 99 won't.

I believe we all have the potential to be a 1, but most will be a 99. Some start as a 1 but end up as a 99. Others start as a 99, but somewhere along the way make a conscious decision to be a 1. Yet others just stay 1's the entire time.

## 1 Will, 99 Won't.

The road to a NCAA Division I conference or the NFL can be a wonderful fulfilling journey filled with experiences and friendships that will last a lifetime. Regardless of how high you set your goals, you can apply that mantra. I hope each and every person reading this will realize your respective dreams. I hope you all work state playoff championships, BCS bowl games or get hired in the NFL some day. It is yours for the taking. I can't help but think that the rosters in the NFL and DI conferences are filled with 1's, not 99's. Without a doubt, once you've achieved the level to which you aspire and you walk out on the field, consider all the time and effort that culminated in that single moment, you will realize you are a 1, not a 99.

**1 Will, 99 Won't.**

# *Zebra Tales*

Don Lucas, Sunbelt Conference Coordinator of Football Officials

*I was in my second or third year in the Southern Conference and I was a Head Linesman. I was working a game where both teams were coached by former NFL players who were actually former teammates on the same NFL team. For whatever reason, it appeared the coaches didn't like each other very much. The game almost got out of hand and I had to flag the coach on my sideline twice for being belligerent and out of control and the back judge had to flag him a third time. At that point in time, once that game was over, we sat down as a crew and talked about it; I realized I came of age during that game. I grew up a lot and learned a lot. I learned you can't go out on the field and just let a coach berate you and your crew to the point where it takes away from the game. No official likes to flag a coach and I'm not suggesting anyone do so routinely. I encourage all officials on my staff to use diplomacy whenever possible but when diplomacy doesn't work you have to take control of the game. I learned a valuable lesson that day and probably raised my standing with my crew and with my coordinator who happened to be at the game that night.*

# Chapter 11

## Overtime: *My Work is Done Here*

T o say I've enjoyed writing, blogging and sharing this journey would be an understatement. I hope you've enjoyed my writing and reflection. I encourage you to pass it on to a fellow official. Direct them to www.profootballreferee.com and have them listen to the podcast. Take pause and appreciate where you are today in your officiating career. Call and thank those that have helped you achieve your current level, in and out of your officiating circles. I'm sure there is a distinguished list behind each and every one of us.

Take an active interest in a new or younger official. Be the mentor they need but are hesitant to seek. Make their learning and advancement easier than yours was. Be a role model, the benefits far outweigh the time and effort. Remember '*The Barrel of Monkeys?*'

The next time you work any football game, do me this favor. Listen to the band play, feel the energy resonating from the crowd, see the intensity burning in the player's eyes. Notice the goose bumps on your arm, the adrenaline coursing through your body, your heart racing as you hear the opening whistle blow the play ready. You've earned the right to be there, it's your moment, your time.

Be the best on the field!

# *More Zebra Tales*

Matt Austin, SEC Referee

*I had an Ohio Valley Conference game where during a scrimmage kick the receiver had returned the ball quite a long way. He was getting close to the goal line and it was almost like the old Fat Albert cartoon. The guys were grabbing and sliding off. The runner was hardly moving at all but he was stil staggering towards the goal line. As he's going to the ground during his last few steps, I'm the referee so I'm straddling the goal line. As he falls the last couple of steps across the line, I signal a touchdown.*

*As I look up, here comes my head linesman running down the sideline shaking his head vigorously side to side. I look at him and yelled, "What?" He replied, "That's not the goal line!" I looked down and I'm standing on the five yard line. So I turned towards the press box and signaled first down. That's just one of those crazy things that happens in a game and proves no one is perfect.*

Wilbur Hackett, Jr., SEC Umpire

*Let me tell you about the incident with Steven Garcia, South Carolina quarterback, a few years ago. I won't elaborate on this much because it's not a big deal and there's nothing bad about it. I think every official needs to protect himself.*

*As an umpire, I can't tell you…and I know if watch enough football and have seen enough officials…you will see some get run over especially umpires in the middle. It's one of those things where I instinctively protect myself every game. I'm probably one of the smallest umpires in college football and I've been very fortunate. I've never been hurt and I've never been knocked out of a game.*

*When that play happened at South Carolina, its just like I told Rogers Redding and I will tell anyone. Its instinct, that's all. No underlying reason, nothing negative, nothing behind the scenes. It just happened on national TV. I just instinctively protect myself and that's what I was doing on that particular play. That's not the first time an official has made contact with a player and it certainly won't be the last. I don't care what position you work, as an official you can get hit and you can get hurt. You have an obligation and a duty to protect yourself.*

Bryan Neale, Big Ten Umpire

*This isn't necessarily a funny story but there's a lesson to it all. We had a Division II game years ago and I was a young second year umpire working with a pretty veteran crew. One team was getting ready to score, I can't recall the down but it was on the one or two yard line. We are counting players and I count twelve men on the field. I count again and I have twelve again. The veteran referee is across the line giving the good eleven signal. So I attempt to count again but before I finish the count the play goes off. I did the proverbial high school move where I ran over the offensive bench to try to hold everyone up so I could count them again but by that time it was too late. They scored a touchdown. So I went to the referee and said, "I'd swear on a stack of bibles we had twelve guys." He said he thought we were okay. We let it go.*

*The scoring team won the game by less than a touchdown. Low and behold, we get the film back and guess what we found? The offense had twelve players on the field. We debated whether or not we should turn ourselves in to the supervisor and we chose not to say anything. Just let them find it. One week went by and we didn't hear anything, another week went by. Nothing.*

*At this point we are thinking, we got that one in the books and lesson learned. Five weeks after the game we get a call from our supervisor that said the team that scored had actually called him and told him they'd scored with twelve players on the field. They wanted to call the league and let them know they didn't do this intentionally and they just discovered it reviewing some film. They thought the league might do some coaching with it. The team actually turned themselves in.*

*Ironically and thankfully, nothing happed to our crew. The lesson learned is that there is nothing wrong with stopping or interrupting a game for something you think is wrong. No matter who you are working with, no matter what level you are working, have the confidence to step up and do what's right - both on the field and off the field.*

# Appendix
## The Evidence

Todd Skaggs, University of Charleston, First Spring Scrimmage

Todd Skaggs, Ryan Kendall, Meddie Kahlegi - WVIAC Brothers

Doug Rhoads, ACC Coordinator of Football Officials

Don Lucas, Sunbelt Coordinator of Football Officials

Bruce Stritesky, NFL Umpire

Dan Foutz, (Colonial, Ivy, Patriot), Blue Ridge Clinic Organizer

Stuart Mullins & Bill Broadhurst (Colonial, Ivy, Patriot)

Stan Weihe (Sunbelt), Roy Potts (SEC), Chuck Russ (SEC)

Dan Gallagher (Big East), Rob Luklan (Big Ten)

Watts Key (ACC), Kenny Long (CUSA), Kip Johnson (ACC)

West Virginia Wesleyan

Sign recovered from the Wesleyan game, gotta love my little brother!

2009 East/West All-Stars Game, Louisville, KY

Dennis Criddle, Todd Skaggs, Alan Grey, Paul Schardein, Andy Faust

2009 Kentucky State Playoffs Crew

Chris Boehlin, Jay Gutterman, Carl "Fuzzy" Klusman, Danny Doyle, Todd Skaggs

The Author Living the Dream

# Appendix B
## The Timeline:
*Journey from High School to College Officiating*

◄━━━━━━━━━━━━━━━━━━━━━━━━━━━━━━━►

October 11, 2008 - Conversation with Tim Bryan about getting into the Mid-South. Hurricane Ike hits Kentucky with 80 mph winds.

October 2008 – Jerry Markbreit speaks at KFOA meeting

November 2008 – I write formal letter of application to Mid-South Assigner, Bob McGrath

December 4, 2008 – Send email to Mike Carey thanking him for inspiring me.

December 5, 2008 – Mike Carey calls me while shopping at Bed, Bath and Beyond. I'm speechless.

December 6, 2008 – I register the www.profootballreferee.com URL.

January 11, 2009 – Dick Honig agrees to be my first interview.

April 2009 – Received invitation from WVIAC's Billy Alton to work University of Charleston Spring Scrimmage (many thanks John Oslica!)

April 25, 2009 – Worked University of Charleston Spring Scrimmage (4 whole plays)

April 26, 2009 – Received email notification of making the WVIAC Supplemental Roster

May 2009 – Attended Heartland Clinic at Ball State University

June 2009 – Training begins for the WVIAC 1 mile fitness test.

July 31$^{st}$ – Arrive for WVIAC Clinic, Wheeling WV

August 1, 2009 – Offered 4 games as Side Judge on Greg Waybright's crew

August 8, 2009 – Greg Waybright assigned as my WVIAC mentor for upcoming season

August 18, 2009 – Worked Glenville State scrimmage

September 5, 2009 – First NCAA game, Walsh vs West Liberty, West Liberty wins big 48-17.

September 12, 2009 – Work Side Judge on Mid-South Conference crew, Newport News vs UVA-Wise

September 19, 2009 – West Liberty vs West Virginia Wesleyan

September 20, 2009 – Moved to Field Judge on Wally Todd's crew

October 5, 2009 – Worked Heartland JV game, Hanover vs Mt. Saint Joe's

October 10, 2009 – West Liberty vs Seton Hill

October 17, 2009 – Glenville vs West Virginia State

October 24, 2009 – 2$^{nd}$ Mid-South game as Umpire, Faulkner vs. Kentucky Christian

October 31, 2009 – Concord vs Fairmont State

November 7, 2009 – Sixth and Final WVIAC game, Concord vs West Liberty

January 1, 2010 – The Referee Nation podcast is born.

February 28, 2010 – Hired as full time WVIAC staff for 2010 season

March 6, 2010 – Attend Blue Ridge Football Officials Clinic, Salem, VA

Early April 2010 – Worked multiple University of Louisville spring scrimmages

April 10, 2010 – Work University of Kentucky spring scrimmage

April 25, 2010 – Work West Virginia Wesleyan Spring Game

May 14-15 – Attend Ohio Association of Football Officials Spring Clinic, Cleveland, OH